diplomatic divide

diplomatic divide

cross-border talks

diplomatic divide

dr humayun khan
g parthasarathy

series editor
david page

LOTUS COLLECTION
ROLI BOOKS

Lotus Collection

© Dr Humayun Khan & G Parthasarathy 2004

This edition first published in 2004
The Lotus Collection
An imprint of
Roli Books Pvt. Ltd.
M-75, G.K. II Market
New Delhi 110 048
Phones: ++91 (011) 2921 2271, 2921 2782
2921 0886, Fax: ++91 (011) 2921 7185
E-mail: roli@vsnl.com; Website: rolibooks.com
Also at
Varanasi, Agra, Jaipur and the Netherlands

Cover design: Sneha Pamneja

ISBN: 81-7436-309-2
Rs 225

Typeset in Minion by Roli Books Pvt. Ltd. and printed at Tan Prints (India) Pvt. Ltd., Jhajjar, Haryana

contents

introduction

relations between India and Pakistan have been at best cool, at worst hostile, ever since 1947. Over nearly 60 years, there have been three major wars between them and a number of serious localized military confrontations, including those over the Rann of Kutch in 1965 and over Kargil in 1999. The disputed territory of Kashmir has been at the heart of their differences and has been the cause of war—declared and undeclared—on two occasions, in 1947 and in 1965. The third major war came in 1971 when India lent its military support to guerrilla forces fighting the Pakistan army in the country's eastern wing to create the independent state of Bangladesh.

Since the two countries exploded nuclear devices in 1998, their long-standing hostility has attracted global attention and prompted serious concern in the international community that their rivalry could escalate into nuclear war and bring disaster to both countries and to the wider region. A sustained period of armed tension and hostility, which began with the Kargil episode in 1999, was only defused in mid-2003 when Pakistan responded positively to a new peace initiative from India. Ambassadors were subsequently exchanged but relations were still far from normal. Restrictions remained on the movement of peoples and goods as well as on the reception of broadcasts across the borders. It was only in the run up to the SAARC summit of January

2004 that flights between the two countries were resumed and only after Indian and Pakistani leaders met at Islamabad that new efforts to resolve their longstanding conflicts were announced.

If governments have found it difficult to build better relations, civil society has not done very much better. There have been a number of important initiatives to stimulate people-to-people contact but these endeavours have been subject to the vicissitudes of diplomatic relations between the two nation states. Many worthwhile contacts have been developed but communication has not been smooth. It has not been easy to obtain visas to visit relatives, let alone for business or tourism. There was a period in the late 1970s and early 1980s when the two governments encouraged visits as an act of policy but obtaining visas has recently been much more difficult. The Consulates General in Karachi and Mumbai, which were intended to facilitate improved cross-border contacts, particularly among divided families and businesses, were closed down in 1993.

In recent years, the internet has become a powerful tool for improved communication, circumventing official restrictions, but its impact remains confined to the computer-using classes. Satellite television has done considerably more to break down barriers among the general public and to give the lie to stereotypes propagated by the state-controlled media in each country. For a generation of Pakistanis, which grew up with no personal contact with contemporaries on the other side of the border, the chat shows and soap operas on Zee or Star have done much to humanize the image of their Indian counterparts. But the flow of images has been largely one-way—from India outwards—and is now much more restricted and controlled because of increased government regulation of cable networks. Moreover, as the coverage of the Kargil war showed, patriotism has its own compulsions even for supposedly independent news media.

Cross-Border Talks is a publishing initiative which attempts to provide a new forum to debate the substantive issues which divide the two countries. There have been many books on Indo-Pakistan relations written by Indian or Pakistani nationals and a number of edited volumes on the subject reflecting different national points of view, but *Cross-Border Talks* is probably the first publishing venture in which eminent Indians and Pakistanis systematically discuss the issues which divide them within the covers of one book.

The series is also distinctive because each volume will be published simultaneously in India and Pakistan to generate discussion in both countries at the same time.

The idea for the series arose in the late 1990s during a discussion in Mussoorie between Pramod Kapoor, the proprietor of Roli Books, and his friend, Professor Francis Robinson of Royal Holloway College, London. Then began the task of finding a Pakistani publisher, developing an editorial structure, deciding on subjects for debate and discovering pairs of authors who wished to develop a dialogue with each other. It has taken time and persistence to make it happen, but with the launch of this volume the idea has begun to take shape.

Apart from the publishers, a number of people have contributed to the emergence of the series, notably Harinder Baweja, who has acted as editorial adviser to Roli Books, Professor Mushirul Hasan of the Jamia Millia Islamia, and I.A. Rehman, former Editor of the *Pakistan Times.* It is above all, however, with a considerable debt of gratitude to the authors themselves that we offer this first volume to the public in the hope that it will contribute in some small way to greater Indo-Pak understanding.

Cross-Border Talks is aimed at members of the reading public in both countries. Its objective is to provide them with informed analyses by recognized experts of the issues which daily occupy the headlines and to explore the barriers to peaceful co-existence. Among the issues scheduled for future debate are the nuclearization of South Asia, nationalism and religion, Kashmir, the growth of fundamentalism, cricket, the legacy of Mr Jinnah, the role of the USA, South Asian culture and economic relations.

The general format for the *Talks* is that the authors agree first on an agenda for discussion. They then write detailed treatments of the subject, which they exchange once completed. At this stage, the authors have an opportunity to revise their texts or to write brief rejoinders. In some cases, the authors decide they do not wish to change their original statements. In others, they take the opportunity to do so. We hope, however, that the debate between them will continue at the launches of the books and that this will engender a wider interest in the subject.

It is appropriate that the series should begin with an overview of bilateral relations by two senior retired diplomats who have acted as ambassadors to each other's countries. Both men had long and distinguished diplomatic careers. Dr Humayun Khan served as Ambassador to Bangladesh as well as to India, and after his return from Delhi took up the post of Foreign Secretary. Mr Gopalaswami Parthasarathy served twice in Pakistan, as Consul General in Karachi as well as High Commissioner in Islamabad. He was also Indian High Commissioner to Australia before taking up his Islamabad appointment. The two men did not serve as ambassadors at the same time. Dr Humayun Khan was Ambassador to India from 1984 to 1988, whereas Mr Parthasarathy was High Commissioner to Pakistan from 1998 to 2000. There was a short period in the 1980s when Mr Parthasarathy in Karachi and Dr Humayun Khan in Delhi were dealing first hand with the same events. However, the value of their exchange lies more in their different perspectives on diplomatic relations over a longer period. Their personal reminiscences throw fascinating new light on the detailed conduct of diplomatic relations during particular crises, as well as offer valuable perceptions of the broad sweep of bilateral relations—why relations went sour and how they might be improved.

The canvas they paint together is a vast one, stretching from the early 1980s to the present day. When Dr Humayun Khan arrived in Delhi, General Zia ul Haq was President of Pakistan, Mrs. Indira Gandhi was the Prime Minister of India, and Soviet forces were still in Afghanistan. By the time Mr Parthasarathy arrived in Islamabad, the Soviet Union had withdrawn from Afghanistan and the Taliban were in the ascendant. At that time, Pakistan was experiencing its fourth elected government in less than ten years, while in India, the Congress Party had recently lost its long-held political dominance and made way for a coalition government under the leadership of the BJP.

The world and South Asia witnessed dramatic changes over those two decades—the end of the cold war, the liberalization of world trade, the growth of fundamentalism and a revolution in communications. All these developments had their influence on relations between India and Pakistan, but some factors remained constant—the unresolved dispute over Kashmir, the growth of military spending, moves towards nuclearization, and the perpetuation of what one of the authors describes as an 'adversarial psychosis'. There were periods when prospects for better relations looked brighter, most notably when the Indian Prime Minister made his famous bus trip to Lahore, but the shadow of Kargil soon intervened and relations plummeted to new depths.

The two accounts provide first-hand impressions of some of the prime movers in Indo-Pakistan relations over this period: Indira Gandhi, Rajiv Gandhi, Inder Kumar Gujral, Atal Bihari Vajpayee, General Zia, Benazir Bhutto, Nawaz Sharif and General Musharraf, as well as the civil servants who advised them. There are graphic descriptions of some significant episodes in bilateral relations: hijacks by Kashmiri separatists, India's Punjab crisis, Operation Brass Tacks, Mr Vajpayee's bus Yatra to Lahore, the Kargil confrontation and the Agra summit. There are also contrasting analyses of the Simla Agreement of 1972, the last comprehensive accord between the two countries, and the on-going Kashmir dispute.

As individuals no longer encumbered by the responsibilities of office, the two men write more frankly for public consumption than they could ever have done as ambassadors. In dealing with governments, civil servants, politicians and acquaintances in their own and in the other country, their accounts are at times candid, critical and outspoken. Sometimes, they differ dramatically in their assessment of key personalities; at other times, they find common ground. But they both acknowledge the depth of friendship and hospitality they enjoyed as ambassadors and the potential for change which greater understanding and cooperation would bring.

Cross-Border Talks also bring out different perspectives on the resolution of Indo-Pakistan divisions. Dr Humayun Khan speaks from a liberal, foreign office viewpoint, which has to some extent been overshadowed in recent years by the growing influence of the Pakistan army in determining foreign policy. His account of the diplomacy in which he was involved in the mid-1980s bears witness to the difficulties of representing a country where power is diffuse and where democratic forces, even when in the ascendant, cohabit with other powerful influences.

Mr Parthasarathy's account, for its part, reflects changes in official Indian perceptions of the Pakistan state and in approaches to dealing with it. As a result of the Kargil episode, there was a detectable hardening of attitudes in New Delhi towards Pakistan and an increased scepticism about the credibility of any Pakistani peace overtures. Though the international community has encouraged the two countries to settle their differences for fear of nuclear war, many Indian strategists have demanded first an end to 'cross-border terrorism' in Kashmir and have taken their cue from the wider 'war on terror' launched by the US administration after 11 September 2001. Mr Parthasarathy's belief that India must deal with Pakistan from a position of strength very much reflects such views.

Ultimately, of course, diplomats are spokespersons ·for governments which themselves reflect the strengths and weaknesses of their respective nations.

Appropriately, both Dr Humayun Khan and Mr Parthasarathy conclude their accounts with reflections on these factors. Both acknowledge that the task of diplomacy is made more difficult by some of the domestic political trends in their own countries, whether the lack of 'internal political equilibrium' in Pakistan or threats to the 'secular and pluralistic ethos' of India. Despite renewed efforts for peace, neither underestimates the danger that the subcontinent could face war again, nor the importance of dialogue to try to avert it. Their preferred diplomatic strategies for their own countries differ widely, but in *Cross-Border Talks* they begin a dialogue which is very much needed at the moment if the two countries are to put the spectre of nuclear war behind them and to ensure a more secure and prosperous future for their citizens.

David Page
Series Editor
January 2004

reflections of an ambassador

dr humayun khan

there is a vast literature on relations between India and
Pakistan, much of it well-researched and well-documented. A
small po rtion consists of writings by practitioners of diplomacy
and one can only hope that much more is yet to come,
particularly from diplomats who have actually served at the
highest level in each others' capitals. If more does come, it is
doubtful that it will reveal many new facts. Journalists,
historians and other scholars have chronicled developments and
events, since the two countries became independent in 1947, in
the minutest detail. Occasionally, former ambassadors have
added a personal view or an inside account which bring a
human flavour to a 55-year saga, characterized by mutual
distrust, periodic conflict, permanent tensions and missed
opportunities. The writings of J.N.Dixit and Rajeshwar Dayal,
both of whom were India's envoys to Pakistan, are good
examples. From the Pakistan side, contributions by
ambassadors who served in Delhi have, by and large, been
limited to articles in various newspapers and journals. Most of
these writings, on both sides, seem to be attempts to put
forward the case in support of the author's own country and its

policies. There is nothing objectionable about this, but arguments and counter-arguments have continued for so long that they have become repetitive and, indeed, something of a bore. Moreover, they tend to detract from the primary objective of trying to find solutions, of promoting mutual understanding and seeking compromises. Indeed, this trading of sterile arguments has, over the years, become an objective in itself, with negotiators on each side concentrating more on scoring debating points than on solving problems. As the overlay of verbiage becomes thicker and thicker, the complexities of each problem multiply and a stage is reached where they all appear to be insoluble.

Despite its abundance, the literature on Indo-Pakistan relations seems inadequate in many respects. One of these is the human interaction that takes place behind the scenes. Yet history is as much the result of interaction between human beings as of the correlation of wider and more sweeping forces beyond their control. Few people are gifted with the ability to place their individual roles in a larger context. Not every man has an eye on history as he lives out his life. But, to paraphrase Nehru, small men do sometimes find themselves in the midst of great events, and even a descriptive account of their own narrow experience might possibly lead to a better understanding and perhaps a different perception of those events.

It is for this reason that I welcomed the opportunity of participating in this venture of publishing a series on *Cross-Border Talks* and writing, together with my friend and colleague from India, G. Parthasarathy, on our reflections as ambassadors in each other's country. He, of course, has the advantage in that he came as India's envoy to Islamabad nearly ten years after I had left New Delhi. Thus, what he has to say is more relevant in today's context. Yet there is a strange continuity, sadly a negative one, in India-Pakistan relations and even a recollection of events and experiences which are more than a decade old could serve a purpose.

With this hope, I am presenting a personal account of my years in Delhi as the ambassador of Pakistan. It is an account that draws entirely on memory. I have consulted no books or documents, nor have I conducted any other research like interviews or discussions. There are no references or footnotes to support what I have to say. No doubt there will be some who can cite hard evidence to show that my version is inaccurate and my analysis faulty. For this I apologize to the reader. I can only give the assurance that this account is as faithful as my memory, whatever that may mean.

The other assurance I wish to give is that I am not undertaking this exercise to present the case for my own country on the various issues between India and Pakistan. When required, I have done that during my career as a diplomat. Now my singular purpose is to try and promote mutual understanding and to strengthen the hands of people of goodwill on both sides who have watched with dismay the suffering, the hardship, the waste of resources, the distrust and the bitterness that the utterly avoidable mistakes and misjudgements of the past 55 years, on both sides, have generated.

In giving this assurance, I must confess that, while not being openly partisan, I do have a nationalistic motive. I firmly believe that it is in my country's best interest to have a good and stable relationship with India. I emphasize this point because self-criticism and admission of faults, especially in the context of an emotion-ridden and sensitive subject like India-Pakistan relations, is seen by some as being unpatriotic. So, to those of my countrymen who may see my views in that light, I would reply that these views are influenced as much by patriotism as by a recognition of realities. Patriotism is in no way enhanced by chest-thumping and jingoism. Nor is it enriched by concealing vested interests in the garb of national interests.

Related to this is the matter of pride in one's country. This is seen as an integral part of patriotism. I have no argument with this, provided pride is limited to holding one's head high and not carried to the point of strutting and swagger. Also, true pride can only arise out of achievement, otherwise it is false pride. By definition, therefore, supporting and endorsing actions and policies that hinder rather than advance economic, social and cultural achievement cannot be called patriotic in the real sense.

I suspect that both India and Pakistan, in their dealings with each other, have often been swayed by the false pride of their ruling elites. Personal and institutional interests have become entrenched and this has resulted in deep-seated mindsets, which now form the single most difficult obstacle to be overcome. In furthering their personal and institutional agendas, the rulers have sacrificed meaningful progress in bilateral relations and denied to their peoples the benefits of lasting peace and of a better life. Criticism of their actions and policies, therefore, cannot be termed in any way unpatriotic. Rather, it becomes a bounden duty.

Coming from those of us who have, for many years, been part and parcel of the so-called policy-making elites these sentiments do, of course, sound somewhat hollow. Why, we may be asked, did you not speak up at the time? How is it that you have only now seen the light? Well, I hope that these reflections will, in however small a measure, show that even among us, there were—in the wilderness perhaps—voices that advocated reason and restraint in the midst of frenzy. At the time, we were dubbed as being soft or defeatist or even naïve. I am not sure that, over the years, these accusations have abated. The constraints of office did not allow public disagreement with the policies of one's own government and the most one could do was to express one's views honestly to one's superiors. Quite often, the impression gained was that these views were respected but when it came to taking crucial decisions, false pride and narrow self-interest rose to the fore, putting in jeopardy the peace and progress which the masses in both countries so badly need. I hope that this personal account will bring out instances where both countries were brought to the brink of disaster by actions influenced by institutional and personal interests rather than the wider national interest.

mission to delhi

Of all the posts open to diplomats of Pakistan, New Delhi is, in my opinion, the most attractive. Professionally, the importance of India-Pakistan relations overshadows all other issues of foreign policy. I would even go so far as to say that India is almost an obsession with Pakistan's policy-makers and whenever an important decision has to be taken, on any front, one of the chief considerations is whether it would strengthen or weaken our position vis-à-vis India. On a personal level, while many diplomats yearn for the glitter of western capitals like Washington, London or Paris, life in Delhi is far more comfortable. Families do not have to make drastic adjustments in their lifestyle. There are no barriers of language, no surprises in food, no wide differences in dress or mannerisms. Above all, Pakistan's envoy to India, like his counterpart in Islamabad, is given an importance that he is unlikely to find anywhere else. He is often consulted by his diplomatic colleagues, sought out by the media and given ready access to the highest circles. All these factors go to make the Delhi post the most challenging and, at the same time, the most enjoyable.

In April 1984, I was working at the Foreign Office in Islamabad looking after the desk in charge of Afghanistan and Policy Planning. This was an extremely busy assignment as we were in the midst of the Geneva negotiations on Afghanistan under the auspices of the United Nations. I did not for a moment imagine that I would be moved for some time. In any case, the normal practice in our Foreign Service was, and still is, that a diplomat is posted abroad for six years then returns home for three before going out again. I had, in fact, been continuously abroad for eight years first as Minister in our Moscow mission, then Deputy Permanent Representative at the United Nations in Geneva and, most recently, Ambassador to Bangladesh. I had returned home in 1982 and was not expecting to go out again for at least another year.

Our Ambassador to India (in 1984, we still had not re-joined the Commonwealth so he was not called High Commissioner) was barely halfway through his tenure, but he was not happy in his post. Rumours of a change in Delhi had been circulating for some time and one of my colleagues was known to have a special interest in it. I was to learn later that his name was actually recommended but President Zia ul Haq did not agree. He took some time to decide and eventually picked me. Our Foreign Minister, Sahabzada Yakub Khan, with whom I had been working closely and who has always been exceedingly kind to me, readily agreed and, to my delight, I was called in and told of my selection.

I might say that though I had never been to Delhi nor was ever considered a specialist on Indo-Pakistan relations, I was no stranger to India or the Indians. I had spent my entire boyhood in boarding at the Bishop Cotton School in Simla where I had made many friends who were now citizens of a different country. In my hometown of Peshawar, in the North-West Frontier Province, my family had forged close bonds with a number of Hindu families. My two older brothers had been educated at the Doon School in Dehra Dun and through them I had come to know many more Hindus. Finally, when I was an undergraduate at Trinity College, Cambridge, I formed new friendships with many Indian contemporaries. At no stage in my youth had I been conditioned to think of them as Hindus or Sikhs or Christians or Muslims. Friendships were forged without prejudice, without motive and without suspicion. I would be going to India, therefore, with none of the anti-Indian feelings that exist among so many Pakistanis.

In the Spring of 1984, when I was told of my appointment, relations between India and Pakistan were showing a rare upward trend. A series of meetings had been held at the level of Foreign Secretaries. The Pakistani proposal for a No-War Pact and the Indian counterproposal for a Treaty of Peace and Friendship were being discussed. The Indian Foreign Secretary, M.K. Rasgotra, came to Pakistan and I, in my capacity as ambassador-designate, attended the talks. The atmosphere was relaxed and friendly and we took our guests up to the hill station of Murree for a night. There the delegations interacted with a good deal of warmth and mutual understanding. Rasgotra was especially pleased after his meeting with President Zia ul Haq who seemed to have convinced him of his sincerity in wanting good relations with India.

There were, however, some faint clouds visible on the horizon. The Indian Army's stealthy occupation of some heights in the Siachen Glacier area had recently been discovered by Pakistan. This was a clear violation of the Simla Agreement of 1972. Under that Agreement the Ceasefire Line, drawn up after the UN sponsored truce in 1949, was converted into a Line of Control, with minor adjustments. The detailed marking of that Line extended only up to a point reference on the map, NJ9842. Beyond that, it was agreed that the Line would run 'northward towards the glaciers': More importantly, however, both sides undertook not to alter the situation on the ground as it prevailed at the time of the Simla Agreement. The Indian move constituted a violation of that pledge and their forces moved a considerable distance westward. In 1984, when the Pakistan army discovered this, few imagined that it would lead to an armed conflict, which has now been going on for 25 years with a heavy loss of life and astronomical costs on both sides

The other worrying situation was the Sikh insurgency in the Indian State of Punjab. During his visit, Rasgotra spoke of suspicions in India that the Inter Services Intelligence (ISI) of

Pakistan was covertly supporting the separatists but, at the time, he appeared to accept the President's assurance that this was not true. He left Islamabad in a positive frame of mind and, as I was to learn later, gave a favourable report to Prime Minister Indira Gandhi, on the basis of which she endorsed the continuation of talks at the Foreign Secretary level.

I arrived in Delhi on a scorching afternoon in May 1984 to be received by a Deputy Chief of Protocol, a very polite young lady from the Ministry of External Affairs, and by all the officials of my own embassy. Contrary to my expectations, there was nobody from the Indian Press and I had to content myself by pontificating at length to the sole representative of Pakistan's official news agency about the high and noble purpose of my mission. This ensured that my words did not reach the audience they were meant for, which was in India! It also showed that, at that moment, there was not too much excitement surrounding India-Pakistan relations. Indeed, even my last call on President Zia ul Haq was devoted entirely to pleasantries and I remember him saying, 'You already know everything, so you don't need any special briefing from me'. He was probably referring to my involvement in policy planning. Perhaps he was too busy with other things to spare more time for me, but he did give the impression of being quite relaxed about relations with India.

I was seeing Delhi for the first time and the old international airport did not impress me too much. The so-called VIP lounge where I sat was a dingy-looking place with dilapidated furnishings, and compared most unfavourably with the ones we had in Pakistan. All this has, of course, now changed. The drive to the embassy residence took me past the modern diplomatic enclave with its magnificent buildings, and I was proud to see that our chancery was the most grand. Then on along broad avenues shaded by old trees, past the famous India Gate to Tilak Marg, where the residence was located. It was a spacious house with vast lawns and a history behind it, because it was once the home of Liaquat Ali Khan, the first Prime Minister of Pakistan. However, it was in a state of acute disrepair and extremely gloomy. This, combined with the oppressive heat, was not the most heartening of beginnings, but the thrill of being Ambassador to India overshadowed such minor disappointments. Within a short time, I was able to get a substantial grant from my government to completely renovate the building, and we moved out to a small flat for the first eight months, while the embassy was transformed into what I believe is one of the best and most comfortable that Pakistan now has. As a matter of pride, I insisted that the marble and all the furnishings come from Pakistan and we commissioned a number of works of art by well-known Pakistani artists. The entire décor was done by a very promising young interior decorator from Lahore who had just started her career.

The moment we had unpacked our suitcases, I started contacting the many personal and family friends we had. They responded with genuine warmth and affection. Many of them were now in high positions in government or the private sector and I found no hesitation on their part to revive the close ties of the past. Emotional and joyous reunions took place and life soon acquired an easy and comfortable rhythm.

On the official side, I had the good fortune to work with M.K. Rasgotra, a cultured and refined diplomat who, as Foreign Secretary, showed unfailing courtesy and kindness towards me, even at the worst of times.

Such times were not long in coming. The goodwill generated by Rasgotra's recent visit to Pakistan was dispelled within two weeks of my arrival when an Indian Airlines plane with a full load of passengers was hijacked by Sikh insurgents and forced to land in Lahore. To deal with the crisis, Rasgotra and I spent 36 hours, without a break, sitting by the telephone, exchanging minute-to-minute information and passing messages to and fro. It was my task to persuade the Pakistan authorities to grant all facilities to the Indian Ambassador, so that he could see at first hand, efforts by our officials at Lahore airport to prevent any harm coming to the passengers and to bring the episode to a satisfactory end. Ambassador Sharma was immediately flown to Lahore in a special aircraft and witnessed the negotiations from beginning to end. I was also asked to get clearance for a team of Indian officials from their Civil Aviation Department to fly into Lahore without visas. My government was reluctant as they felt that it was the responsibility of our officials to negotiate the release of the passengers and their task would become greatly complicated if Indian officials intervened. Eventually I managed to obtain this concession but, to my chagrin, I discovered much later that the Indian team included one of their top Intelligence operatives. This was my first direct experience of the unpleasant reality that, no matter what the degree of cooperation may appear to be on the surface, there are always undercurrents of mutual distrust which translate into various forms of trickery. While Rasgotra and I were absolutely open with one another, there were agencies in each government that would never accept this openness as genuine.

This particular episode ended satisfactorily with no harm coming to the passengers and the hijackers surrendering to our authorities. Within 36 hours, all the passengers were flown back to Delhi in a specially chartered Pakistan International Airlines Boeing. The Indian aircraft returned separately. I was at the Delhi airport to receive the passengers and there I was given a muted word of thanks by the Indian Minister of State for Foreign Affairs. Rasgotra was more effusive in his gratitude for my government's cooperation. But this was only part of the story. That same evening I attended a dinner at which Mrs Gandhi was the guest of honour. I was seated at the same table as Rajiv Gandhi and some Indian Ministers. Naturally, I expected some expression of relief and perhaps of appreciation and goodwill. Throughout the evening, however, not a word was said about the successful resolution of the hijacking crisis. Mrs Gandhi pointedly ignored me.

A few days later, I paid my introductory courtesy call on her. Such occasions are normally for introduction and, at most, general statements about wanting to promote good relations. The new envoy expects a word of welcome and some friendly personal enquiries about his family and his own career. Mrs Gandhi wasted no time on any of these.

She received me, not with a handshake or the normal Indian *namaste*, but with the traditional Muslim greeting of *aadab arz*, somewhat raising my expectations. Her first sentence, however, took me aback. With a wry smile, she said, '*Aap ke aatey hee hadsa ho gaya*', meaning 'As soon as you arrived a mishap has taken place.' Quite nonplussed, I looked at the diplomat who was her aide and mouthed the question, 'The hijacking?' He nodded, whereupon I made an effort to highlight the positive aspects of the episode, like the rescue of the passengers, the arrest of the culprits and the cooperation between officials of both countries at Lahore airport. She cut me short to say, 'But you did not allow our people to meet the hijackers or search their luggage.' Naturally, I was thrown a bit off balance by the Prime Minister's directness and even more by the long silences that followed her opening remarks. I managed to say a few words about my determination to work for better relations and the clear instructions of my government to that effect. She spoke only one more sentence, 'We have never been against good relations.' The interview lasted seven minutes, one minute longer, I was later to learn, than that given earlier to the new Japanese ambassador. She clearly was a woman of few words with little time for niceties.

In due time, I was to discover that, although Rasgotra had given her a positive account about the role of the Pakistan officials in the hijacking drama, her ambassador in Islamabad had sent in a highly negative report. It said that he had received little cooperation and was not kept fully in the picture from moment to moment and that, generally, the conduct and the motives of the Pakistani officials, during negotiations with the hijackers, were dubious. Apparently, his suspicions were aroused when our officials spoke over the wireless with the Sikh rebels in a friendly manner but he did not realize that, if the passengers were to be saved from harm, the hijackers had to be kept in good humour.

Following this unfortunate event, there was a short spell of comparative calm. Rasgotra and I continued to try and keep the normalization process on track and were making preparations for the next round of discussions which was to be held in Delhi. A while earlier I had presented my credentials to President Giani Zail Singh in a very impressive ceremony. The Chief of Protocol came to my residence in the morning and drove with me to Rashtrapati Bhavan in an open limousine. It was a scorching day and I was most uncomfortable in my black woollen *sherwani* (long coat). Luckily, it was a short drive to the magnificent palace designed by Lutyens. There I was presented a smart guard of honour and then led up the stairs lined with the President's Bodyguard, resplendent in their scarlet and gold tunics with starched turbans. The ceremony took place in the grand durbar hall where British viceroys were sworn in and it was relatively short. I simply handed over a copy of my speech with my credentials to the President, after which there was an official photograph. The President then led me to a smaller chamber where we talked in general terms. In marked contrast to my meeting with the Prime Minister, this one was exceedingly warm and when we joined the other guests for tea, Gianiji spent a good deal of time talking to my wife and daughters, inviting them to visit the gardens of Rashtrapati Bhavan whenever they wished.

crisis in punjab

This period of relative calm was extremely short-lived. Within days, on 6 June 1984, Mrs Gandhi ordered military action against the Sikh insurgents in Indian Punjab. Operation

Bluestar, as it was named, saw the storming of the Golden Temple in Amritsar, where the rebel leader, Jarnail Singh Bhindranwale, with hundreds of armed followers, was ensconced. Few observers in Delhi, including the diplomatic corps, imagined that she would take such a drastic step. I do not think any of our own Intelligence agencies foresaw it. I do, however, remember the Turkish ambassador saying to me, a day or two earlier, that military action was being contemplated and I expressed total disbelief. It was difficult to imagine that Mrs Gandhi would make such a dangerous move. In a sense, Jarnail Singh Bhindranwale was her own creation. It was well known that she had, the previous year and on the advice of her then Home Minister, Giani Zail Singh, encouraged him in an attempt to split the Akali leadership, which was vigorously agitating for the implementation of the Anandpur Sahib Resolution. This included a number of Sikh demands such as asking that Punjab should be given the city of Chandigarh as its capital and extensive water rights in the rivers flowing through its territory. But Bhindranwale turned out to be a more determined and more violent opponent of the government than any of the other leaders and, by the summer of 1984, the Punjab had become a virtual battlefield with daily killings which led to a large migration of Hindus from the State.

Operation Bluestar turned out to be a veritable bloodbath with casualties exceeding those at the infamous Jallianwalla Bagh massacre in 1919. The figure quoted in Delhi at the time was in excess of 3000, including about 500 Indian Army personnel. What was worse, the holiest of Sikh shrines had been brutally violated with tanks driving through the temple gates and with considerable damage done to the Akal Takht and the Harminder Sahib, the most sacred structures in the compound. The library and the religious archives, which included documents written in the hand of the Gurus, were destroyed and many innocent worshippers who were staying in the temple rooms perished. But it was not so much the physical destruction as the emotional trauma inflicted on an entire community that now dominated the political scene in India. The tension was palpable.

There was little doubt in my mind that Pakistan's suspected involvement with Sikh rebels would now be exploited to the full, but I did not expect that it would come from a military source. On that very evening while the temple was still smouldering, Major-General K.S. Brar, who led the attack, appeared on television and claimed that weapons and ammunition bearing Pakistani markings had been recovered and that among those killed were a number of Pakistani nationals. This latter conclusion was based on physiological evidence which could not possibly distinguish between Muslims from different counties, including India. No accusation of direct involvement in the tragic incident was made officially by Rasgotra, but he did call me in on more than one occasion to tell me, in no uncertain terms, that his Prime Minister was furious with Pakistan's official media for its biased reporting and particularly with our television for beaming inflammatory programmes to Indian Punjab.

The direct consequence of her anger was that she broke off the dialogue at the official level a week before our delegation was due in Delhi. Years later, Rasgotra told me that he had advised against this but she was adamant, preferring to rely on negative reports from her Intelligence agencies and her ambassador in Islamabad. Thus, the normalization process was brought to a halt, but thanks largely to Rasgotra's positive approach, he maintained regular contact with me. When the occasion demanded, he did not mince his words, but his elegance and his good manners never deserted him and he constantly assured me that he would continue to work for a restoration of the dialogue.

During these anxious times I returned to Pakistan to report in detail about my discussions at the Indian Ministry of

External Affairs and the prevailing mood in Delhi. I highlighted the point that the Indians were convinced of our active support for the Sikh insurgency and of the close involvement between some of its leaders and our Inter Services Intelligence (ISI). At the meeting with the President and his senior Ministers these remarks of mine were received in silence, but with the observation that the Indians were exaggerating. I agreed to the extent that I saw the problem in Indian Punjab as essentially an internal, political one and found no substance in the claim that had it not been for external support, it would not have reached the proportions of a crisis. The Indians knew this, yet insisted on diverting attention to Pakistan's involvement.

I remember that an American Congressional delegation came to Delhi in the summer of 1984. One evening, the US Ambassador called me and said he wished to come to the house and discuss an important matter. He told me that the Indians were emphasizing to their visitors that were it not for Pakistan's involvement in the Punjab, the process of normalizing relations between the two countries could go forward, but they saw no point in talking to Pakistan while this involvement continued. In other words, they wanted Pakistan to present a 'clean chit' as a precondition to a dialogue. I pointed out to Ambassador Harry Barnes that the Indians were perfectly aware of the history of Indo-Pak relations, one of the permanent features of which was that if one country was in any sort of difficulty, the other's natural instinct was to exploit and add to those difficulties. On no occasion had either country chosen to act as a good neighbour and refrained from capitalizing on the situation. The most obvious example was the Bangladesh crisis. Similarly, whenever Pakistan had problems in its Sind province or along the border with Afghanistan, the Indians made extra efforts to add fuel to the fire. It was, therefore, unrealistic to demand a 'clean chit' as a precondition. The adversarial psychosis on both sides was, in itself, the root of the problem and the prime purpose of any dialogue should be to address this. A positive change could only be a result of a dialogue, not a precondition to it.

It was this same theme that I kept hammering in my meetings with Indian officials. Though I denied our support for the Sikhs, these denials convinced no one. I think they realized that I was not totally aware of the reality on the ground and my denials were not evidence of my perfidy. The argument that the best way to remove suspicions was to talk about them certainly found favour with Rasgotra and, indeed, with his successor, Romesh Bhandari. But it cut no ice with Mrs Gandhi. She chose to rely on the advice of her more hawkish advisers. In any case, to divert attention to Pakistan in the midst of her internal difficulties was too great a temptation to resist.

Despite my ignorance of the exact nature of ISI's activities in the Indian Punjab and despite President Zia's public stance of reasonableness towards India, I could not help but conclude that there were forces in Islamabad that believed India's discomfiture in the Punjab worked to our advantage and we should add to it. Acting on the basic assumption that India's ultimate aim has always been to destroy Pakistan (an assumption I have never subscribed to) they argued that internal unrest in a border state weakened the enemy's military bridgehead and consequently reduced the danger of an invasion. This is quite understandable in a country which is obsessed with its security. The problem arises when this obsession leads to equating military doctrines with national policy and this is a mistake which seems inevitable in a country which has been ruled by the army for the major part of its existence. It was extremely difficult for me, as a civilian functionary, to sit in meetings with powerful military figures and to argue that unrest in the Indian Punjab might not be in Pakistan's interest. It was self-evident to me that a larger and more powerful neighbour which is on edge could be a greater danger than one which was at peace with itself and that the temptation to externalize internal problems would be overwhelming because even the most divided of nations tend to rally around the flag to meet an outside threat. But all these arguments ran contrary to the military mindset that Pakistan's response must be calibrated against the yardstick of Indian capabilities, not her intentions. The worst intentions had to be assumed, so any factor which hampered the enemy's capabilities was an advantage to Pakistan.

In the midst of Indian suspicions about our role in Eastern Punjab and the palpable tension in Delhi between Hindus and Sikhs, I was still able to go about my duties without fear or hindrance. I moved around unescorted and there was no let-up in my contacts with Indians. Soon, however, there was another hijacking and, once again, the aircraft was forced to land in Lahore. This time, the Pakistan authorities refused to let it stay, but they did refuel it and permitted another technical landing in Karachi before it was flown to Dubai. The authorities there not only rescued all the passengers, but arrested the hijackers and promptly handed them over to India. This showed Pakistan up in a bad light and it was alleged that our government had tried to persuade the UAE not to hand them over. Another more sinister dimension appeared when some of the passengers, among whom was the well-known defence analyst K. Subramaniam, revealed that when the aircraft was first hijacked soon after leaving Ludhiana in India and before it landed at Lahore, the hijackers were unarmed but, immediately after take-off from Lahore, one of them had produced a pistol. This immediately led to the accusation that the firearm had been provided by our agencies at Lahore airport. Romesh Bhandari, who had by now replaced Rasgotra as Foreign Secretary, informed me that the weapon had been handed over to the Indian authorities at Dubai airport and they were determined to trace its origins. I passed this on to Islamabad and was instructed to firmly deny that Pakistan had any hand in the affair. In fact, a day or two later, President Zia personally rang me up on the open line to say that he had spoken to Mrs Gandhi and stressed to her the need to beef up security at Indian airports because the hijackers had succeeded in smuggling the pistol aboard at Ludhiana. The Indian government followed their investigations with great vigour and thoroughness and many months later, indeed after I had left New Delhi, obtained proof directly from the supplier in Germany that the pistol had been originally sold to an official agency in Pakistan. I am still not sure that President Zia was aware of this. He certainly showed great displeasure when the evidence finally proved our involvement. Fortunately, interest in the matter had, by then, greatly abated but the disclosure certainly did our credibility little good.

All these developments added to Mrs Gandhi's ire so that, by September 1984, there was open talk of her taking retaliatory action against Pakistan. I recall being told by Mark Tully, the highly respected BBC correspondent in Delhi, that military action on a limited scale in Kashmir could not be ruled out and that the months of October and November would be crucial.

As if to confirm this, in early October, while I was leading the embassy cricket team in a match at the Chelmsford Club, I was urgently called away by my Defence Attaché. He told me that he had information from a Grade A-one (that is, undeniable) source that India had decided to break off diplomatic relations with Pakistan. My colleague, Riaz Khokhar, who was later to become High Commissioner in Delhi and is now Foreign Secretary, advised me not to rush into anything but look for other signals, but the Defence Attaché was absolutely certain of his source. Somewhat rashly, therefore, I passed on the information to our Foreign Office where it naturally caused a great stir. Much to my embarrassment the report turned out to be untrue.

Then, on a sunny morning at the end of October, as I sat in my office attending to routine work, one of my colleagues rushed in with the news that Mrs Gandhi had been shot outside her residence by one of her bodyguards and was lying in a critical condition at the All India Institute of Medical Sciences. His own private information was that she had already succumbed to her injuries. I immediately contacted President Zia's Chief of Staff and asked him to pass on the message to the President, who was visiting Peshawar.

We learnt that the body would lie in state for two days at Teen Murti House, formerly the residence of India's first Prime Minister, Jawaharlal Nehru. I called all my senior colleagues and told them we would go together to pay our last respects. When I suggested that we might say a small prayer for the departed soul as we passed the bier, one of the military attachés objected on the grounds that this would be un-Islamic. My reaction was one of disgust, but knowing how strong his religious feelings were, I did not press him. Next day, we walked as a team, conspicuous in our national dress, past crowds of mourners who were genuinely overcome with sorrow and showed no sign of hostility towards us. For the moment, the nation's anger was turned upon the Sikh community because the identity of her assassins was public knowledge They had been arrested on the spot. Both Beant Singh and Satwant Singh were members of her personal bodyguard. Her security advisers had strongly opposed keeping Sikhs in that position after the massacre in Amritsar, but she had rejected their advice in a grand gesture of secularism.

Within hours of her death, rampaging mobs of Hindu extremists, prominent among whom were allegedly members of the ruling Congress Party, started an orgy of killing, burning and looting in which many innocent Sikhs lost their lives and their property. It was common talk in Delhi that the mastermind behind the riots was a Cabinet Minister. From the roof of my house, as the sun was setting on that fateful day, I was able to see spirals of smoke rising in the distance, though the area in which we lived was quiet and deserted. The violence continued for three days until finally the army was called in to restore order.

I was extremely worried about my many Sikh friends, and one of my concerns was what I would do if any of them sought refuge in our embassy. I knew of some prominent personalities among them who had moved to European missions. I was quite clear in my mind that I would give them shelter but they were far too considerate to put me in an awkward position. In any case, it would only have increased animosity towards them if they turned to the Pakistan embassy because it was only a matter of time before somebody sought to implicate us in the assassination of the Prime Minister.

As soon as the announcement of the official funeral was made, President Zia ul Haq telephoned me to say that he would personally attend. I received a long list of his entourage and called him to request that he should not bring more than six persons as the Indian organizers would be fully stretched. He readily agreed.

The funeral was a massive affair and, as was to be expected, something of a shambles. Many years later I saw Sir Dennis Thatcher in London and mentioned that we had met briefly on that occasion. His retort was: 'Ah! The Gandhi funeral. Wasn't that the most brilliantly organized—ah—cock-up you ever saw!' The Indian protocol officers, no doubt in shock, got everything from transportation to seating arrangements horribly mixed up. At one stage, as all the front row seats were filled up and Princess Anne was still looking for a seat, a junior official walked down trying to unseat someone by asking, 'Excuse me, are you a Head of State or a Head of Government?'

The crowds were not as large as expected because of the tense law and order situation in Delhi, but the significance of the event and the enormity of the tragedy was not lost on anyone. The numerous leaders who had come to Delhi used the opportunity to meet bilaterally and many of them held discussions with President Zia. He showed his uncanny personal skills when Mrs Thatcher asked to call on him. This was in accordance with diplomatic protocol because he was a

Head of State and she a Head of Government. He, however, insisted that he would call on her and did so at the residence of her High Commissioner. I was struck by the fact that the British Prime Minister, who for years had objected to the military dictator even setting foot in her country, was now full of praise for him, not only for his Afghan policy but for what he was doing in Pakistan itself. He gave her a long explanation on the necessity of non-party elections in Pakistan, and she let him have his say. Clearly, Zia's role in Afghanistan had completely changed his image in the West just as, many years later, the horrific events of 11 September 2001 would do for General Musharraf.

From our point of view, the most important meeting was with the new, young Prime Minister of India, Rajiv Gandhi. The two met privately for nearly an hour while we all sat in an anteroom. Zia himself dictated a memorandum of the conversation as soon as he returned to his hotel. It clearly indicated that the prospects for putting bilateral relations back on track held some promise.

Rajiv Gandhi had, since the death of his brother Sanjay, moved to his mother's side and into politics with some reluctance and devoted his time largely to Congress Party affairs, though there was some suggestion that he had his own coterie, which advised his mother on government policies. Overtly, however, he seemed to have little or no experience of government. He was virtually forced into the Prime Ministership because national elections were only weeks away and his Party wanted to garner the sympathy vote. He was in a mould different than his mother. Exceedingly polite, soft-spoken and with fine human instincts, he was more akin to his grandfather though, of course, without his giant intellect. In his own unassuming way, he soon let it be known that a generational change had taken place and that he was not burdened with the baggage of the past. Unlike his mother, he held no ingrained animosity towards the military regime in

Pakistan. He was fascinated by gadgetry and his first priority was the technological modernization of India rather than its regional dominance. By temperament, he was conciliatory and free from prejudice. Later evidence was to show, however, that because of his lack of political and administrative experience, he often yielded to his close advisers many of whom were steeped in the old ways or were whiz kids with grandiose ideas.

As expected, the sympathy vote did give Congress a comfortable victory in December 1984. The new Prime Minister, now elected in his own right, immediately set out on a path of reconciliation with the Sikh community. His innate modesty showed when I congratulated him on reaching an accord with Sant Longowal and said it showed courage on his part to take such a risk. He replied 'My risk is not half as great as the one Santji has taken.' Prophetic words, because the Sikh leader was assassinated not long afterwards. Tragically, a gentle soul like Rajiv Gandhi was himself to meet a violent end some years later because of past policies on another front, the Tamil issue with Sri Lanka. That too, in my view, was an instance of a mild and well-intentioned leader paying the ultimate price for departing from policies which promoted violence and strife.

calmer waters

India-Pakistan relations entered a relative period of calm after Rajiv became Prime Minister, though lurking suspicion about Pakistan's involvement in the Sikh insurgency and, indeed, in the assassination of Indira Gandhi remained. Foreign Secretary Romesh Bhandari broke a long stalemate by going to Pakistan and resuming talks with his counterpart. He had been brought up and, like Rasgotra, educated in Lahore and there was a marked sentimentality about his visit to Aitchison College and Government College, both of which he had attended. He also had numerous personal friends with whom he renewed contacts. I, too, had known him for a long time and he had shared rooms with my eldest brother at Trinity College, Cambridge. I remember that he once summoned me and informed me that two members of my clerical staff in Delhi were being declared persona non grata and expelled as they had been caught engaged in espionage. My response was that, while I could not question India's right to take such action, I would not like the incident to affect the process of normalization which had been put back on track with great difficulty. The Indian decision, I said, was regrettable but I wanted to avoid any escalation, hence I would advise my government not to retaliate, although that was the established custom. Appreciating this, Bhandari displayed that not uncommon contradiction between the personal and the professional which characterizes Indo-Pak relations by advising me not to stick my neck out too far.

Romesh Bhandari retired within a year and went on to higher things. He was succeeded by A.P. Venkateshwaran, in whom I found a fine gentleman, devoid of any prejudice or ill-will. He was candid, easy to talk to and had an endearing warmth about him. I recall one summer, when I was on leave in London, he tracked me down to telephone and say there had been an unfortunate incident where a servant of our Air Attaché had been manhandled in the street by some Indian Intelligence operatives. He wanted to apologize personally to me for this. It was a highly unusual thing to do, as normally such incidents are officially denied, but that was the kind of person 'Venky' was. Soon afterwards he was to pay for his straightforwardness by being summarily removed from his post. To his credit, the entire Indian Foreign Service rose to his defence but, true to his gentlemanly character, he quietly retired. Fortunately, his successor was another distinguished and experienced diplomat, K.P.S. Menon, whose father had served in Baluchistan before Partition, and who was also totally free from any anti-Pakistan prejudices.

During the early part of Rajiv Gandhi's premiership, a number of high-level exchanges between the two countries took place. Foreign Minister Sahabzada Yakub Khan came to Delhi for a meeting of the Joint Ministerial Commission. His sophistication and skill were met equally by the good manners and charm of the Indian Prime Minister. At the official reception at Hyderabad House, Rajiv Gandhi left the receiving line to specially come and congratulate us because he had just received the news that Pakistan had beaten India at cricket in Sharjah with Javed Miandad hitting a six off the last ball of the match.

Dr Mahbubul Haq, Minister for Finance and Planning, led a delegation to India and spoke eloquently about 'reaping a harvest of goodwill'. He initiated moves to expand trade relations and, soon afterwards, the Indian Commerce Minister visited Islamabad to pursue the matter. With broadminded representatives like Mahbub and Secretary-General Ejaz Naik from Pakistan and V.P. Singh from India, the prospects were bright indeed. One senior bureaucrat from our side was vigorously opposed to any agreement but he received a severe dressing down from President Zia and the decision to expand the list of items for trade was taken despite his strong objections.

Other exchanges at the official level included a women's delegation to attend a meeting of the South Asian Association for Regional Cooperation in Delhi and an unusual visit by a group led by the Governor of West Punjab, Makhdoom Sajjad Hussain Qureshi. A gifted conversationalist with an unmatchable sense of humour, the Makhdoom had a hilarious session with Giani Zail Singh, the Indian President. They both spoke in Punjabi, the language common to them. The conversation included a number of witty asides about a shy young man accompanying the Governor whose name was Nawaz Sharif and who had obviously come along for fun. Speaking of the improvement in India-Pakistan relations

Gianiji, with uncanny accuracy, observed, *'Khambey te lug gaey, par bijli hali nayeen chali'* (The poles are up but the electricity has not yet started to flow).

More important than the official exchanges were those at the people's level. I had the pleasure of hosting hundreds of Indian friends at musical recitals by renowned Pakistani vocalists like Mehdi Hassan, Ghulam Ali, Farida Khanum, Reshma and Abida Parveen. These events generated enormous goodwill and positive interest in Pakistan. I was besieged with requests for videotapes of Urdu dramas aired by Pakistan television and our visa section was flooded with applications. With the full support of our Secretary-General Interior, Roedad Khan, I was liberal in issuing visas and sometimes we issued almost a thousand in a single day. In one case, the Indian Foreign Secretary personally rang to recommend a certain individual. On investigation, I found that his name was on the blacklist drawn up by our Interior Ministry. I rang up Roedad Khan and said I proposed to grant the visa despite this. He unhesitatingly authorized me to go ahead.

A most significant event was the Golden Jubilee celebrations of the Doon School, India's best known elite educational institution, where Prime Minister Rajiv Gandhi had himself been a student. More than 80 'old boys' from Pakistan with their families came to attend. I participated in the celebrations as much in my capacity as Pakistan's Ambassador as the brother of two former school captains. The reunion was a highly emotional one and speeches by Kemal Faruqui and my eldest brother, Afzal Khan, were given standing ovations. When Rajiv Gandhi addressed the gathering at the formal opening ceremony, every reference to the visitors from Pakistan was loudly cheered. Later, the Headmaster held a special reception and the Indian Prime Minister spent the whole afternoon with them. On their return from Dehra Dun, more than 200 Indians, many of whom had reached high positions in the public and private sector, attended a gala dinner given by me at the embassy. The evening was redolent with nostalgia, with goodwill and conviviality.

Following this, there were visits by Indians who had attended Aitchison College, by golf teams, by railway officials, by ladies who studied at Kinnaird College, Lahore and many others. Though not of direct political significance, these exchanges carried the very important message that there were many people in both countries, people of influence, who wished to play a part in improving relations.

Most important was the regular exchange of journalists. The Indian Press at that time, as indeed always, included men and women of great distinction and repute and it was my privilege to know many of them. Few developing countries could boast of a galaxy that included, at the time, names like George Verghese, Bhabani Sen Gupta, Inder Jit, Pran Chopra, Inder Malhotra and Kuldip Nayar, apart from those grand old doyens, Khushwant Singh and Prem Bhatia. Each of them added to my knowledge and my understanding of the Indian scene and each, in his own way, tried to contribute to a better understanding between our two countries.

There were many other sources of encouragement also. A number of very senior retired armed forces officers showed keen interest in promoting good relations with Pakistan and the older ones among them spoke affectionately about colleagues across the border with whom they had served together in the British Indian Army. I remember especially Major-General Mohinder Singh Chopra, then in his eighties and a contemporary of Field Marshal Ayub Khan who, together with his whole family became our closest friends, saying to me that he had but one wish left in life and that was to visit his old regimental centre in Abbottabad in the Northwest of Pakistan. He was delighted when I was able to arrange this and the Frontier Force Regiment, the famous Piffers, gave him the highest protocol.

No less valuable was the encouragement and support I received from retired diplomats and civil servants whose views carried great weight. Many of them have since passed on but, during my tenure, they gave me constant support and were always ready to talk to me candidly about relations between our two countries and ways of improving them. Men of great distinction like B.K. Nehru, a bon vivant and an imposing personality who combined all the social graces with a wealth of experience and a strong commitment to principles. Once he came to dinner at my house driving his ancient Mercedes. When he was leaving, it would not start so I called out my domestic staff and joined them in pushing it. As the engine burst to life, B.K. Nehru leant out of the window and shouted: 'I am writing my autobiography and I must describe how the Pakistan Ambassador himself pushed my car.' His delightful book appeared many years later, though without any mention of this incident, and was a pleasure to read. P.N. Haksar, a highly cultivated and handsome gentleman, had about him an intellectual arrogance which seemed in every way justified. He always saw things in the widest historical and philosophical perspective and his observations had a rare originality about them. Kewal Singh, former High Commissioner in Pakistan and Foreign Secretary, was the epitome of courtesy and actively engaged himself in promoting understanding between India and Pakistan, as did Rajeshwar Dayal who had an outstanding career both as an Indian and as an international diplomat. These were, like so many others, public servants of whom any country would be proud.

Among politicians, despite occasional grandstanding for public consumption, I found many with a genuine commitment to peace and a readiness to explore all avenues towards this end. Some were more forthcoming than others, some had blind spots but, as politicians, many showed vision and a deep understanding of the dynamics of Indo-Pakistan relations. Because of their long experience of democracy and debate, they were skilful practitioners of their art. Regrettably, politicians in Pakistan have not had the same opportunities, so the depth of their knowledge and understanding of international relations and of statecraft is not half as impressive.

During my years in Delhi, I gained enormously from my discussions with political leaders. As with other categories, I am fully conscious that mention of some names may seem invidious, but as these are personal reflections, I venture to do so with the full awareness that I might be omitting many others that also merit recognition.

As I have indicated earlier, I found Mrs Gandhi studiedly cold and uncommunicative. On the few occasions that I tried to converse with her, she did not encourage me. It has to be remembered, of course, that she died only six months after my arrival in Delhi and these were by no means the easiest days of her life. After Operation Bluestar, she was in constant personal danger and her security was extremely tight. She was no longer able to move about freely or mingle at gatherings. I first saw her when she attended a concert in May 1984 and I was greatly impressed by the lack of protocol and the simplicity of the arrangements. She arrived alone in a small Indian car and walked in like any other guest, took her seat and later moved about greeting and talking to many people. After 6 June 1984, however, she could never travel without three or four decoy cars and a host of security officials. Strong woman that she was, she continued to relentlessly and with some ruthlessness pursue her own political agenda. With the Punjab still in flames, she created further problems for herself in Kashmir by insisting that the Governor dismiss the elected government of Farooq Abdullah. Governor B.K. Nehru, who was her cousin, refused to take this unconstitutional step and was summarily removed. He was replaced by Jagmohan, who was commonly referred to in Delhi as a hatchet man, and the elected leader of the state was replaced by G.M. Shah, thereby creating a very unstable situation in Kashmir. She also manipulated the removal of N.T. Rama Rao in Andhra Pradesh because she suspected him of trying to build a unified opposition to her regime. Beset as she was with serious internal problems, it was no wonder that she had little time for the Pakistan Ambassador. Nevertheless, I got the clear impression that she had a strong animus against the military regime in Pakistan and she did not trust General Zia ul Haq. Nor for that matter had she liked Z.A. Bhutto, whom she branded a liar and a fraud.

Her son, Rajiv Gandhi, who was a gentleman to the fingertips, also did not talk very much but was never discouraging. I was greatly flattered when, on the occasion of my farewell call on him before returning to Islamabad as Foreign Secretary, he graciously said, 'Now with you there I am hopeful that things will further improve.' I was always impressed by his noble instincts but he was still finding his feet.

Narasimha Rao, who was Foreign Minister for a while and then became senior Minister handling a number of important portfolios, was always cordial and correct but non-committal. V.P. Singh, first Commerce and then Defence Minister, was a leader always open to reason but had about him a sort of dignified reserve. Another member of the Cabinet, N.K.P. Salve was informal and friendly and, because he was in charge of cricket in India I always enjoyed his company. For the same reason, my conversations with President Venkataraman, an avid cricket fan, gave me much pleasure.

But it was my interaction with political leaders who were then out of office that I found most informative and fruitful. Atal Bihari Vajpayee, whose BJP was then in the doldrums was, nevertheless, a highly respected figure. He showed a most enlightened approach towards Pakistan and, some years earlier, as Foreign Minister in Morarji Desai's Cabinet had succeeded in raising bilateral relations with our country to a new plane. I was greatly impressed by his wisdom and his cool-headedness. It is a tragic irony that, many years later, India-Pakistan relations should have reached their lowest ebb during his Prime Ministership. I, for one, remain convinced that history will credit him for having genuinely tried to prevent this. Even as I write this, there is evidence to show that he has not totally given up his efforts for peace and amity between the two neighbours.

I would say the same about my good friend Jaswant Singh who, during my time, was a member of the Rajya Sabha but who later became the Foreign Minister and Finance Minister. I saw in him a man of keen intellect, a great nobility of character and an impressive command of the English language. Some in Pakistan have accused him of being arrogant. He is not, he is just dignified and polished. I am convinced that he shares with Atal Bihari Vajpayee a deep-seated and genuine desire for good relations with Pakistan. He was always forthright and honest with me, even more so after I retired and he was in high office. Each time I met him I came away more impressed by his objectivity and his sincerity. I am sure that one of his great regrets will remain that he was unable to put India-Pakistan relations on the right track before he left the Ministry of External Affairs.

If ever I met a politician with gravitas, it was Raja Dinesh Singh, once a close confidant of Mrs Gandhi, who inducted him into the Cabinet for the first time. He returned as Foreign Minister in the late 90s but his health failed and India was prematurely deprived of an outstanding public figure. He and his family showed great friendship and affection towards us and his death was a personal loss. He was always wistful about the uneasy relationship between India and Pakistan. Careful with his words, he came across as a progressive but disenchanted individual who kept his emotions in check.

By contrast, Inder Kumar Gujral never tried to conceal his emotional commitment to Indo-Pakistan amity. He revelled in nostalgia and went out of his way to cultivate personal relationships with people who came from Pakistan. He too, like many others, was to feel frustrated. I like to believe that the Gujral Doctrine he later propounded was a genuine attempt to break away from the hide-bound attitudes of the past. I think he was quite right in saying that India, as the largest country in the region, should not demand full reciprocity for every gesture made towards its smaller neighbours but should show large-heartedness. Unfortunately, the implementation of this doctrine in its initial stages extended to other neighbours and aroused suspicions that it was never intended to apply to Pakistan.

A great honour for us as a family was the friendship we received from Mrs Vijaylakshmi Pandit, sister of Jawaharlal Nehru. She invited us to her house in Dehra Dun and spent much time talking to my daughters. She was obviously never happy with Indira Gandhi but was supportive of Rajiv. On Pakistan, she seemed to have an open mind and she paid a visit there, returning very pleased with the reception she got. Another memorable pleasure came from the personal contacts we had with Indian film celebrities. Raj Kapoor and his family were legends in India and, because he came from Peshawar, he made it a point to befriend us and have us meet all of them. Screen legend, Dilip Kumar, whose real name is Yusuf Khan, also belonged to Peshawar and always met us warmly and talked nostalgically about his hometown, where he soon returned to receive an unprecedented welcome.

Finally, I must mention one very special individual on whom I relied a great deal when I was ambassador. Mohammed Yunus, affectionately known as 'Chacha' (Uncle), was almost a part of the Nehru family and close to three generations of Prime Minister, Jawaharlal, Indira and Rajiv. He belonged to a merchant family of Peshawar and, early in life, committed himself wholeheartedly to the Congress Party. His elder brother married the daughter of Khan Abdul Ghaffar Khan, Frontier Gandhi as he was often called or Badshah Khan as he is known among the Pathans. Chacha Yunus never reconciled himself to the partition of British India and in 1947 chose to become an Indian citizen. This did not endear him to people in Pakistan and he never visited his birthplace for nearly 50 years, though he had a large number of relatives across the border and kept in close touch with them. In a sense, we too had a distant family connection with him because one of my wife's aunts was married to the youngest son of Badshah Khan, Abdul Ali Khan, who served as Principal of Aitchison College and later Vice-Chancellor of Peshawar University. So, Chacha Yunus treated us like family and we were often in each other's homes. Later in this narrative, I shall recall an important occasion when his assistance was highly effective but, generally speaking, he provided me with a channel through which I could convey our point of view directly to the highest authority in India. This did not always have the desired effect but it was, nevertheless, a great asset.

It was during my tenure that Badshah Khan paid his last visit to India and stayed with Chacha Yunus. I remember telling President Zia that his son, Khan Abdul Wali Khan, would also be coming and that, although he was an opponent of the government, we had old family connections and I would be meeting him regularly. Without hesitation he said that not only should I meet him, but I should provide any assistance that he needed. He later directed me to fly to Bombay, where Badshah Khan had been hospitalized, and to convey his best wishes for a speedy recovery with flowers on behalf of the President. The veteran leader returned to Delhi where I again went to see him. I was, in fact, the last visitor he was able to see because that very afternoon he went into a coma from which he never recovered. He spoke clearly but his memory was obviously failing, because he kept naming members of my family and asking if I knew them.

I have not seen any man command as much respect and affection in India as Badshah Khan. When he arrived, Rajiv Gandhi and senior members of the Cabinet were at the airport to receive him and the young Prime Minister visited him regularly during his illness. But the grand old man had little time for protocol and ceremony. He came with one change of clothing, sitting in a wheelchair pushed by his grandson, and seemed totally indifferent to the honours being done to him.

He rarely spoke, but when he did, he had no hesitation in telling the Indians how they had failed to live up to the high ideals of the freedom struggle. Not once, during their stay in India, did he or his son Wali Khan, say a single word that was critical of Pakistan or its government. He was eventually flown back unconscious and passed away soon afterwards. The news reached Delhi at around eight in the morning and by ten o'clock Rajiv Gandhi, accompanied by a large party, set off for Peshawar in a special aircraft to attend the funeral rites before the body was taken to Jalalabad for burial. This was Rajiv's first-ever visit to Pakistan but he did not have any official engagements. It was also the first visit in over 40 years by Chacha Yunus, thus breaking a long self-imposed exile. Once the ice was broken, he was able, much to his relief, to return regularly to be with his family.

To return to the narrative, 1985 saw the convening of the first SAARC summit in Bangladesh. There, our President and the Indian Prime Minister met for the second time, the first having been at Mrs Gandhi's funeral. Although SAARC has made little substantial headway since its establishment in the early 1980s, it has one great benefit in that it enables the leaders of South Asia to meet face-to-face on an annual basis and sometimes this provides an opportunity for breaking deadlocks in bilateral relations. Strictly speaking, bilateral issues are excluded from the formal discussions but they are conducted on the sidelines, particularly during the Retreat where the leaders meet in an informal setting without aides. On the river cruise in Bangladesh, Rajiv Gandhi told President Zia that one of the conspirators in the plot to assassinate his mother was reported to have been given shelter in Pakistan. Zia assured him that he would have the matter investigated and Rajiv, without any bitterness or rancour, left it at that. This, I thought, was an example of a leader with a deeply personal complaint not allowing it to affect decisively his attitude towards his counterpart.

The President was proceeding on a State visit to Sri Lanka straight from Dhaka and Rajiv invited him to stop over in Delhi on his way home. Though the visit lasted only a few hours, intensive one-to-one talks were held before lunch and again in the evening. The atmosphere was relaxed and friendly and a number of decisions were taken to give an impetus to the normalization process. In some cases negotiations were already under way but the imprimatur of the highest authority gave them a welcome push. The Defence Secretaries soon met to discuss the Siachen problem, the Interior Secretaries took up the question of cross-border incursions and drug trafficking, the hotline between the two army headquarters became more active and water experts started talks on the controversial Wuller Barrage, which the Indians proposed to build on the river Jhelum in Kashmir. By 1986, the two sides were actively engaged in a multifaceted dialogue.

The most important outcome of President Zia's visit was a totally unexpected one. When the two leaders emerged from their private session in the evening to join their delegations for refreshments, Rajiv casually asked the President if it would be a good idea for the two countries to enter into an agreement not to attack each other's nuclear facilities. For a moment Zia was taken aback, but he quickly recovered his composure and enthusiastically welcomed the proposal. The Indians had played this issue very close to the chest and at no stage during the preparations for the summit had this subject been raised. The nuclear issue had, of course, been in the forefront for some time, with political and media circles openly voicing concern at Pakistan's progress on this front. During my annual address to the Indian National Defence College, I was mercilessly grilled about it. On our side, fears were being openly expressed that India, perhaps in collusion with Israel, was planning to attack our installations at Kahuta near Islamabad. In these circumstances, Rajiv's almost by-the-way proposal was in fact highly significant. Working out the details took three years and in December 1988, I had the privilege of signing the accord on behalf of Pakistan. Rajiv Gandhi also gave us a small lesson in democracy when, the matter having been agreed, he excused himself from escorting his guest to the airport where they were to hold a joint Press conference. He said he must first report to Parliament, which was in session, before he made a public announcement. The Press conference was handled with great skill by both leaders. Inevitably, one correspondent asked whether Kashmir had been discussed. It was Zia who immediately replied, 'We will come to Kashmir when the time is right.' I must admit that the progress we were making on so many fronts was largely because President Zia did not allow the intractable issue of Kashmir to block all other paths.

I do not wish to suggest that he did not give primary importance to the issue but, tactically, he decided to put it on the backburner. He was, however, not totally inactive on the ground and there is reason to believe that he initiated the ISI's activities inside Kashmir which, in due course of time, were to become the main cause of friction between India and Pakistan and were to lead to a sharp deterioration in relations signified by the present situation.

kashmir and the simla accord

Nobody can deny that right from the beginning, the Kashmir dispute has been at the heart of differences between the two countries. Today it is in the forefront more than ever and appears to have become an insuperable obstacle in the way of any genuine improvement of relations. It is futile to argue that it is anything less than the single substantive issue that blocks progress and, with the widely differing positions of the two sides, the prospects of a solution appear bleak indeed.

The traditional Indian approach has been that overall improvement of relations will facilitate a peaceful solution of Kashmir. The Pakistan view has been that, without a solution of

Kashmir, no meaningful progress can be made on the broad front. The one occasion when the positions were reversed was at Simla in 1972, where Mrs Gandhi was keen to settle Kashmir once and for all, but Zulfiqar Ali Bhutto called for progress on other fronts as a first step. A compromise was reached when Bhutto agreed to converting the Ceasefire Line established by the UN in 1949 into a Line of Control. Each side undertook to respect the control of the other in their respective areas, pending a 'final solution' to be sought through bilateral negotiations. Mrs Gandhi relented at the last minute and did not insist on making the Ceasefire Line, with minor adjustments, the permanent international boundary. Many of her advisers were unhappy at the time and claimed that she had missed a golden opportunity. This was still the view of many when I arrived in Delhi 12 years later.

What exactly happened at Simla remains something of a mystery. I was not in the Foreign Office at the time, and my observations are based on detailed discussions with some of the participants, both in Delhi and in Islamabad. The Pakistan version is that it was a diplomatic triumph for Bhutto, because, with literally no cards in his hand, he was able to preserve his country's position on Kashmir, to regain 5000 square miles of occupied territory in West Pakistan and to pave the way for the release of 93,000 prisoners of war being held in India since December 1971. The inclusion of phrases like 'without prejudice to their well-known positions' and 'commitment to the United Nations Charter' which appear in the text of the Agreement, negate in Islamabad's view, the interpretation that a de jure change had taken place with the mutual acceptance of the Line of Control or that the United Nation's resolutions on the subject had been superseded by the agreement to seek a bilateral solution.

The Indian interpretation, as I was repeatedly reminded in Delhi, was different. They claimed that Mrs Gandhi made a last-minute concession at Simla for a number of reasons. Firstly, she was impressed by the argument that an imposed solution based on a military victory would only mean that Pakistan's enmity with India would become permanent and defeat the underlying purpose of establishing a durable peace. A number of people in Delhi told me that this was the argument pressed by P.N. Haksar, her chief adviser, who strongly maintained that it would be unwise to force a Versailles-type settlement on Pakistan. When I called on him in New Delhi, Haksar said much the same thing to me. It would be foolish on the part of either side, he said, to believe that the Kashmir problem could be solved through the use of force. If anything, this would widen the gulf between the two countries and lead to permanent ill will. The then Foreign Secretary of India, T.N. Kaul, was, or so I learnt in Delhi, of a different mind and left Simla early under the impression that no accord could be reached. The second factor was that both the United States and the Soviet Union had brought strong pressure on Mrs Gandhi to reach a mutually acceptable settlement. They had earlier cooperated in stopping her from continuing the war against West Pakistan after her victory in the East in 1971. They now combined to dissuade her from imposing a unilateral settlement. Another important factor was that Bhutto had taken with him to Simla a number of Opposition leaders from the smaller provinces of Pakistan, including Arbab Sikander Khan Khalil, Governor of the North West Frontier Province and Ghous Baksh Bizenjo, Governor of Baluchistan. Some of them had been stalwarts of the All India Congress before Partition and had worked with Mrs Gandhi's father. She held them in high esteem and had specially brought Mohammed Yunus with her to Simla to act as a link with them. Through him they sent private entreaties to Mrs Gandhi not to send Bhutto back empty-handed and to give democracy in Pakistan a chance. They themselves had entered into a power-sharing arrangement with him a few months earlier and decided to cooperate with him. Soon after Simla, they helped him get his new Constitution unanimously passed by the

National Assembly. Within six months, however, he forced their elected governments in two provinces out of office and, not long afterwards, put the leaders of their parties behind bars. Like them, at Simla, Mrs Gandhi decided to put her faith in Bhutto. He convincingly argued that given enough time, he would be able to bring public opinion in Pakistan around to accepting the Line of Control, with marginal adjustments, as the permanent international boundary. Some of those present at the time, told me in Delhi that he said to her, '*Aap mujh pe bharosa rakhen*' (you must have trust in me). He maintained that, if he was seen as having yielded to pressure, the Pakistan army, defeated though it might be, would have his head.

There was also much talk in Delhi when I was there that, in fact, Bhutto had a verbal agreement with Mrs Gandhi that the proposals he was making were in the nature of an interim agreement, hence the language in one clause of the Simla Agreement that a 'final' solution would be reached at a later meeting between Heads of Government. There is no hard evidence to prove this allegation about an oral understanding. It is nevertheless true that it did not suit either leader to put anything like this in writing. Mrs Gandhi would face domestic criticism that despite India's unassailable position at Simla, she had relinquished the claim to a large part of Kashmir while Bhutto would have little chance of political survival in Pakistan.

In spite of their divergent interpretations of the Simla Agreement, both parties continue to pay lip service to its centrality in the context of Kashmir. The difference is that, while India calls for a settlement in accordance with Simla, Pakistan prefers to cite, 'The Simla Agreement and the relevant resolutions of the United Nations.'

By and large, this Agreement has held the field till now and, in the opinion of some, averted an armed conflict for 30 years. This is perhaps an oversimplification because many other factors have since entered the equation. Anyway, it cannot be said that either side has stuck unswervingly to the letter and the

, spirit of the accord. The Indian occupation of Siachen was the first open violation. Many years later, Pakistan undertook the misadventure in Kargil. Both these violations resulted in armed hostilities which, mercifully, did not expand beyond a local scale.

The spirit of Simla clearly commits both sides to working for a peaceful solution of Kashmir. It also states that such a solution should be sought through bilateral negotiations. The Pakistan case that the bilateralism clause does not in any way rule out other peaceful methods authorized by the UN Charter may be legalistically arguable but it is not exactly in keeping with the underlying spirit of the accord. Clearly, both sides agreed to give primacy to the bilateral course. But that was only laid down as the procedure of first preference. There is nothing in the agreement that changes the substantive position of either side, unless one accepts the argument that the establishment of the Line of Control was the initial step in a direction which would be followed through to a final conclusion by making it the permanent international boundary. The Indian position that a solution can only be reached through bilateral negotiations also appears to me to be excessively rigid. After all, the bilateralism clause itself allows for 'any other method mutually agreed upon'. Surely, if bilateral negotiations have failed for 50 years, it may be time to agree on some other mutually acceptable procedure. Indeed, in recent years, India has itself invoked international intervention on an issue which has become central to the Kashmir dispute, the issue of 'cross-border terrorism'. It is most unlikely that any solution suggested by a neutral party would give either side all that it claims, nor would it ignore the ground realities. Some sort of workable compromise would be suggested and it would be less difficult for both sides to entertain a compromise proposed by a third party. Neither side, on its own, will find it easy to initiate moves towards a compromise, even though it is clear that no solution is possible without one.

Today, the Kashmir dispute appears to have become more intractable than ever before and, indeed a greater threat to regional and global stability than it has ever been. Yet, over the years, subtle movements have taken place. For example, since the mid-90s, whenever a dialogue has been initiated, the Indian formulation of the agenda has included a special mention of Kashmir as one of the subjects to be discussed. This constitutes a significant departure from the past when any specific reference to Kashmir as a dispute was anathema to the Indians. As for Pakistan, it still insists on the primacy of Kashmir, but now seems ready to discuss other aspects of normalization alongside it. The trouble starts when talks actually begin. India says, 'Let us tackle the easier issues first and then move on to the most difficult one.' Pakistan says, 'No progress is possible on other issues until we solve the main problem.' These are, of course, extreme positions and prevent negotiations from taking off. Past experience has, however, shown that different rates of progress can be attained on different issues and this progress should not be cast aside lightly. My own view is that even the most intractable issues can be resolved more easily in an overall atmosphere of cooperation and even the easiest issues are unlikely to be resolved in an atmosphere of confrontation. Perhaps a compromise will one day be reached when all issues will once more be put on the table but more urgent and intensive focus will be maintained on Kashmir. The basic starting point must be that both sides should realize that it is in their long-term strategic interest to cooperate and live peacefully with each other. Specific disputes can then be addressed with the broad understanding that both sides wish to preserve an overall relationship of peace and cooperation. There are numerous examples in the world where countries have taken this strategic decision and fashioned their policies accordingly. They have proceeded to improve relations on a broad front with countries with which they have serious differences on specific issues. China continues to work for good relations with the US despite the question of Taiwan. Similarly, it is improving its relations with India in spite of their boundary dispute.

Of course, the Kashmir dispute has now become qualitatively different from others in that it has acquired an intensely emotional dimension and has become deeply enmeshed in the domestic politics of both India and Pakistan. It has been the cause of repeated armed conflict; it has seen much bloodshed, enormous economic costs and blatant violations of human rights. Worst of all, it has created vested interests that are powerful enough to thwart any attempts at a reasonable compromise. With the complexities of the issue multiplying over the years, it becomes more and more difficult for any leader in either country to accept compromise and to survive. This is particularly true of Pakistan. It would take a Sadat or a Rabin to break the deadlock, and the consequences could well be the same as those two brave men faced. Behind the scenes, a number of possible solutions have been debated, but the issue is so emotionally charged that backdoor diplomacy, though always helpful, would probably not win popular support if it produced anything in the nature of a surprise. Unfortunately, so far, neither side has made any effort to influence public opinion towards an ultimate compromise. In fact, they have both encouraged hardline thinking and sought to make political capital out of maintaining rigid positions. The conundrum, therefore, remains that though most people in both countries want a peaceful solution, their leaders publicly encourage them to favour the all-or-nothing attitude.

Developments on a number of fronts have had both positive and negative effects on the Kashmir issue. The nuclearization of South Asia has rendered it an infinitely more dangerous flashpoint. Though there are many advocates of the so-called 'balance of terror' thesis who argue that nuclear weapons diminish the chances of conflict, I am convinced that the potential risks far outweigh the illusory sense of security that nuclear weapons provide. The one positive side to this is that the international community does not underestimate these risks and is now paying more attention to the situation. It has to be more proactive in this regard because both India and Pakistan want good relations with the industrialized nations, particularly the United States, and might be ready to listen. When I was in Delhi, the nuclear debate was just hotting up. At that time, Pakistan was in the dock for its clandestine efforts to acquire weapons capability. Despite its nuclear test at Pokharan 1 in 1974, India seemed to have convinced the international community that its programme was entirely peaceful. The US media and Congress were targeting Pakistan and the Indians happily joined the chorus. Ironically, it was India that was to become the first to break the barrier in 1998, forcing Pakistan to do the same. In the mid-80s, the first signs that the nuclear factor was entering the India-Pakistan equation were surfacing and India focused its attention on getting the US and the West to lean on Pakistan. Covertly, however, India was itself moving fast towards weaponization and knew perfectly well that Pakistan was in no way ahead.

International opinion too was more focused on non-proliferation generally and not specifically in the context of Indo-Pakistan rivalry. The result was that interest in disputes between the two countries was not immediate enough to encourage intervention. Today, that has changed and there is great concern. Hopefully, this will result in greater international efforts, which could be most helpful in reaching a solution of the Kashmir dispute.

The other important factor of very recent origin is, of course, terrorism—which is today at the centre of the world's concerns. It was barely talked of in the 1980s and then only in local contexts. After 11 September 2001, it is an international issue. Any form of violence which targets innocent people is defined as terrorism and there is no clear distinction made between those engaged in freedom struggles and terrorists. The latest stalemate between India and Pakistan is based on this issue with the Indians insisting that 'cross-border terrorism' must stop before any talks can be resumed. Pakistan is under heavy international pressure to curb the activities of what it calls freedom fighters operating from its side of the border. This was never a good policy anyway, because one thing has always been clear: India is never going to come to terms under pressure of force. Pakistan has tried this more than once with disastrous results and it might be in its own best interest to voluntarily abandon these methods.

operation brass tacks

By the summer of 1986, I was into my third year in Delhi and, on the surface, relations between the two countries were showing a slow but steady upward trend. The Indians were by then more preoccupied with the Tamil crisis in Sri Lanka. Pakistan had moved on to a quasi-civilian form of government with Mohammed Khan Junejo as Prime Minister. He had no previous experience of India nor any contact with Indian leaders, so there was something of a hiatus. Despite the apparent calm, I had a lurking feeling that it did not necessarily reflect a deep and unambiguous commitment to good relations. The adversarial mindset on both sides was still there and the traditionalists could not resist the temptation of indulging, whenever the opportunity arose, in the rhetoric that had become a part of their political idiom. President Zia, whose intentions were always difficult to fathom, consistently refrained from making inflammatory statements and Rajiv Gandhi was both soft-spoken and restrained. This mutual restraint had filtered down to the official level as well. I was specifically told by the President that, if the necessity for strong language arose, I should not be the one to use it but should leave it to Islamabad. Prime Minister Junejo, too, was cool-headed and not in the habit of making harsh statements, but I did notice that some of his Muslim League colleagues still believed that domestic political mileage could be gained from adopting forceful anti-India postures. To some extent this began to be reflected in official statements by the Foreign Office, where press briefings were held every Wednesday afternoon and, for me, Thursday mornings became a somewhat anxious time when the Indian press reported these statements.

Towards the end of 1986, the SAARC Summit was convened in Bangalore. The Indian delegation, led by Rajiv Gandhi, spent most of the time in bilateral negotiations on the side with the Sri Lankans and the multilateral agenda took second place. Prime Minister Junejo represented Pakistan. He was an unknown figure in India and, to my intense embarrassment, the local authorities in Bangalore had hung up hundreds of banners with pictures of the seven Heads of Government but they displayed General Zia instead of Mr Junejo. He saw these banners as he drove in from the airport, but it was a measure of his graciousness that he never raised the matter with me. I have known of cases where ambassadors have had to pay a heavy price for mistakes for which they are in no way personally responsible.

Despite his preoccupation with Sri Lanka, Rajiv Gandhi had an extended bilateral meeting with our Prime Minister in which they covered a wide range of issues. The Pakistan side, acting on information from its army, raised the question of a large military exercise which India was planning to hold in Rajasthan, barely 50 miles from the border. Despite an existing agreement on the sharing of information in such matters, Pakistan was apprehensive about the scale of these manoeuvres and the purpose behind them. Rajiv replied that his army wanted a 'big tamasha' (a grand show) but that he himself was not in favour of spending so much money and wanted to cut down on the expenditure. He assured Mr Junejo that it was nothing more than a training exercise and he hoped the hotline between the two military headquarters would be used to remove any doubts or suspicions.

At the embassy we had, of course, kept a close watch on the preparations for the exercise, code-named 'Brass Tacks' and my Defence Attaché constantly assured me that nothing untoward was happening. A week or so before the manoeuvres began, there was a somewhat strident statement about Pakistan which the Indian Press attributed to defence sources. I telephoned Foreign Secretary Venkateshwaran and said such statements only added to our misgivings. He soon called me back to say he had spoken to the Defence Ministry and advised against saying anything that may raise tensions. We came to know that Brass Tacks would involve six divisions (some writers later mentioned a higher figure) of the Indian Army including mobile formations and armour. We also learnt that, for the first time, live ammunition would be used and that coordinating movements by the navy and the air force would be practised. Despite all this, my Defence Attaché was convinced that no war-like preparations like cancellation of leave, call-up of reserves or movement of back-up forces to other border areas were being undertaken.

Because of the daily reassurances from my defence advisers, I was quite relaxed and also took comfort from the fact that Brass Tacks had aroused no particular excitement among the diplomatic community. Nor had I received any indication of alarm from Islamabad. It was a great surprise, therefore, when the British High Commissioner rang me up on the evening of 23 January 1987 to say that he had just returned to Delhi after a tour and had heard disturbing rumours that there was 'some sort of a problem' on the border. Rather naively, I assured him that there was no basis for such rumours and he expressed great relief. Almost immediately thereafter, I received a call from the Ministry of External Affairs that Minister of State, Natwar Singh, wished to see me at 7.30 next morning.

Natwar Singh had been Ambassador to Pakistan and was an expert on the subject of India-Pakistan relations. He knew me well, as he did most senior Pakistani diplomats and politicians.

Whenever we met, he was informal and friendly. On that morning, however, he had a stern expression and my initial attempts at bonhomie fell absolutely flat. He sat me down and said he had a most important and urgent message to be conveyed to my government. He then took out a piece of paper and read slowly from it so that I could write it down verbatim. It was a sombre message which stated that the Pakistan Army had moved two divisions, including an armoured division, from their peacetime locations in the Multan and Gujranwala areas to the Punjab border. India regarded this as an offensive move and, unless these troops went back to their peacetime locations within 24 hours, India would be compelled to move its own forces to the border 'for purposes of defence'.

I was astounded by this ultimatum. How could it be, I thought, that such a sudden development could take place with no prior indication to me from Islamabad that a crisis had arisen nor any warning from me that Brass Tacks was more than it seemed to be? I remember it was a Friday, a holiday in Pakistan, so the first priority was to ensure that my telegram would be read immediately. I telephoned the senior-most officer in charge of the India desk and asked him to go to the cypher room immediately. Having done this, it occurred to me that the quickest and most reliable way to find out Rajiv Gandhi's views was through Chacha Yunus who had immediate access to him. I went to his house and asked him to speak to the Prime Minister. He agreed to do so.

That same morning, an East European Head of State, I think it was the President of Bulgaria, was arriving in Delhi on a State visit and the entire diplomatic corps was required to be present at the airport. Normally, in the midst of such a crisis, I would have foregone such a ceremonial duty but I was hoping that I might get a chance to speak directly to some high Indian functionaries. The first person I caught sight of at the airport was the Chief of Army Staff, General Sundarji. I had always found him easily approachable so I had no hesitation in going up to him and asking what he thought of the situation. He replied that Brass Tacks was nothing more than it was proclaimed to be, the largest annual training exercise of the Indian army. He was conscious that it would cause some concern in Pakistan and when he learnt that our 1st Armoured Division, which was on manoeuvres east of Multan, decided to extend those manoeuvres, he well understood this as a cautionary measure and gave it no further thought. However, when overnight this Division moved North and took an offensive position on the Punjab border, which was lightly defended, and this was accompanied by troop movements from the Gujranwala-Kharian area, he had no option but to warn his government that counter-measures must be taken. He again reassured me that there was no sinister agenda behind Brass Tacks.

Prime Minister Rajiv Gandhi was also at the airport and when the ambassadors filed past shaking hands with the high dignitaries, he smilingly said to me, 'Zara temperature neechey laana chaheyeh' (We should bring the temperature down a bit). I quickly replied that I had spoken to General Sundarji and would immediately report to my government. As the line of diplomats was moving fast, there was no time to have a more detailed exchange.

As we were leaving, the US Ambassador took me aside and said he had been summoned to the Ministry of External Affairs in the middle of the night and informed that a serious situation had arisen on the border and that the Indians were compelled to take necessary counter-measures. He knew that the Soviet Ambassador had also been called in and given a similar briefing. Both of them, he went on to say, had since received instructions from their governments to urge restraint on the Indians.

Immediately on my return to the office I sent off a telegram giving details of my conversations at the airport and saying these further strengthened my conviction that there was no hidden motive behind Brass Tacks. It would, I wrote, be a tragedy if a conflict were to erupt merely because of suspicion and a lack of communication. I urged that our Vice Chief of Army Staff, who was de facto in command of the army while President Zia continued to hold the office of Chief of Army Staff, should telephone General Sundarji as this would clear the air immediately and decisively. Much later, I was to learn that General K.M. Arif, responded to this suggestion by saying he would do so if the Prime Minister ordered him but personally he thought this would be a sign of weakness. (This has recently been confirmed by General Arif in his book *Khaki Shadows*). I also went back to Chacha Yunus, who said he had contacted Rajiv Gandhi and driven with him to the airport that morning. Rajiv had told him to assure me that India had no hidden motives, but that the troop movements by Pakistan to the highly sensitive Punjab border was not something they could ignore. A while later, I met Defence Minister V.P. Singh at a ceremony and discussed the situation with him. He gave me similar assurances.

Once again I fired off a telegram conveying all this to Islamabad. This time, I went on to suggest that Mr Junejo should speak directly to Rajiv Gandhi over the telephone and I was confident that the crisis would be quickly resolved. The only reply I got was that I should inform the Indians that Pakistan was ready to enter into discussions at any level to find a peaceful resolution of the crisis.

Meanwhile, throughout the day on 24 January, the Indian official media highlighted the movement of Indian forces to the Punjab border and the tone was distinctly aggressive. With some diffidence, particularly as I had no information as to the situation on the ground nor about the deployment of our troops, I decided to call a Press conference on the 25th. In this I was grilled intensively about the exact disposition of the Pakistan army, a subject on which I was totally ignorant. At one point I was directly asked whether they had crossed the river Sutlej and were now positioned to its east. I replied that the river ran partly through our own territory and crossing it was not the issue. I could only assure them that we would not be the first to cross the Rubicon. I went on to speak of my government's offer to resolve the crisis through discussions at any level and then, rather hesitantly, I threw in the comment of the Indian Prime Minister at the airport the previous day that he was also in favour of bringing the temperature down. This disclosure caused quite a flutter, given the overtly strident tone of the official media over the previous 24 hours.

I learnt later that among the gathering at the press conference, there were two representatives of the Indian Intelligence who promptly informed the office of the Prime Minister of this disclosure. His office then issued a directive to the official media to project matters in a way that showed that it was India which had initiated steps to defuse the crisis. I have no absolute confirmation of all this, but this is what I was told privately later by a friend who worked in the Office of the Prime Minister. Anyway, I noticed a sudden change in the tone of Doordarshan (the government-run television channel) that very evening and there was a visible softening. Just before the official banquet for the Bulgarian President, I was summoned again by Natwar Singh. His demeanour was noticeably less stern. Though the demand for troop withdrawals remained, there were clear indications that the situation could be contained.

The next day was India's Republic Day, the occasion for a grand parade along Rajpath, the old Kingsway. In Islamabad, I was later informed, Mr Junejo was in constant session with the Defence Committee of the Cabinet and the Service Chiefs. Unexpectedly, General Zia ul Haq attended the evening session and posed a direct question whether we were in fact ready to go to war and bear all the consequences. Fortunately, the response was not too enthusiastic and sane counsel prevailed. President Zia then endorsed my earlier suggestion that Mr Junejo should speak personally to Rajiv Gandhi. So, on the morning of 26

January, the call was placed. There was quite a flutter when the reply came that the Indian Prime Minister was not available and, I believe, some of our hardliners began saying that it was never a good idea to telephone because we should have known we would be snubbed. A few hours later, Rajiv Gandhi returned the call to say that he was attending the Republic Day parade and hence was not available in the morning. From there on, there was no difficulty in the two leaders agreeing to talks at the Foreign Secretaries' level to de-escalate the situation.

My relief, as can well be imagined, was immense. That afternoon, there was the President's Republic Day reception at Rashtrapati Bhavan and I vividly recall standing with the Indian Prime Minister and Natwar Singh, with the entire diplomatic corps at a distance in a semi-circle, watching anxiously as we talked. We briefly reviewed the events of the past two days and Rajiv Gandhi remarked, 'I hope everything will be cleared up when Sattarji comes.' His reference was to Abdul Sattar, Foreign Secretary of Pakistan.

Next afternoon, to relieve the tension, I went to play golf at the Delhi Golf Club. The first person to come up and embrace me was the Deputy Chief of Staff of the Indian Army who jokingly remarked, 'Thank goodness, it is all over. You chaps ruined our golf by having us on red alert for the past two days.'

As I have said, it is not my primary intention to contradict other versions of the Brass Tacks episode. I have merely given a narrative account of what happened before my own eyes in Delhi during those fateful hours. My references to what happened in Islamabad are based on what I was told later by colleagues because, at the time, most of my telegrams went unanswered. It was the closest that the two countries had come to war in 16 years and I still shudder to think that hostilities could have broken out on the basis of mere suspicion and misunderstanding. Accidental wars are as lethal as deliberately planned ones and they remain a constant risk between India and Pakistan.

There are many in Pakistan, particularly in military and Intelligence circles, who claim that the tactically bold military step of moving our forces to the Punjab border gave the Indians cold feet and they were forced to abandon the true objective of Exercise Brass Tacks. The more I have thought about this, the more difficult I find it to accept this thesis. In January 1987, there was no immediate causus belli. The Kashmir issue, which in one way or the other occupies centrestage in conflicts between the two countries, had been on the backburner for more than 15 years and neither side seemed eager to bring it to the forefront. The situation in the Indian Punjab had cooled down considerably and, from India's point of view, was continually improving as a result of Rajiv's conciliatory policies. Anti-Pakistan feelings on this score had considerably abated. India was more than occupied with the problem in Sri Lanka and its armed forces were engaged on that front. Above all, Pakistan's standing on the international stage was still high because of its role in Afghanistan. It was the darling of the so-called free world as it supported the mujahideen against the Soviet occupation and their struggle was still at a high pitch. At the same time, hopes of a détente between the two Cold War rivals were increasing and Gorbachev's unease at the continuing Soviet involvement in Afghanistan was becoming apparent. The last thing either superpower wanted was a major flare-up in South Asia which would revive their rivalry. Some have suggested that it was fear of Pakistan's nuclear capability that finally brought India to its senses. This view was given some credibility because of a totally unnecessary interview given to an Indian journalist by Dr A.Q. Khan, often referred to as the father of Pakistan's atom bomb, in which he said that his country already had nuclear weapons capability. Rajiv Gandhi had, in response, proclaimed in the Lok Sabha that this did not frighten him as India itself was only 'a turn of the screw away', should it decide to go nuclear. I do not think this factor, at that time, decisively influenced the denouement. It can safely be assumed that India was fully aware of the stage at which Pakistan's nuclear programme had reached and did not need Dr A.Q. Khan to tell them. In any case, the argument does not hold water, because if India feared possible nuclear retaliation, it would hardly have planned an attack under the guise of a military exercise in the first place.

Looking at all these factors, I could see little reason for India to embark on an invasion without any cause and, in retrospect, I have no reason to change the assessment I made at the time. It is, however, very difficult to contradict Intelligence agencies who always have sources of information which are unavailable to others. If their predictions come true, they can take full credit. If their predictions do not come true, they can claim that their timely warning was the reason. Nor is it easy to challenge the logic of the military mind which postulates that you must look at the enemy's capability, not his intentions and act accordingly. Given the ingrained belief that India's permanent objective is to destroy Pakistan, this logic naturally holds sway and no one, I suspect, will ever convince the Pakistan army that it was not its bold tactical move that prevented an Indian attack in January 1987. These are the dangers of equating military doctrine with national policy, and I fear that this approach will continue to constitute a serious risk as long as the army remains the final arbiter. It is still not clear whether the forward positioning of Pakistani troops at that time was authorized by the civilian government of Mr Junejo or even by President Zia ul Haq, who, after all was also the Chief of Army Staff. In any event, when it came to the crunch, it seems it was his intervention that saved the day.

All this is not to say that the Indian side can be absolved of blame and, indeed, some Indian analysts have accused General Sundarji and the young Minister of State for Defence, Arun Singh, of having created an unnecessary crisis. There is some evidence to show that Rajiv Gandhi's instructions to cut down on the scale of Exercise Brass Tacks were circumvented and perhaps even Defence Minister V.P. Singh, was unaware of this. There is also considerable evidence that the Indian Army Headquarters were not nearly as forthcoming in providing prior information to their Pakistani counterparts as they were supposed to do under an existing agreement. My own assessment of General Sundarji was that he was a brilliant and innovative commander. He had about him that special panache which is traditionally associated with cavalry officers. It was typical of him, for example, to order the use of live ammunition in a training exercise and to test coordination with the navy and the air force. He was a strong advocate of mobile capability and he sought to reform the Indian army into a fast moving force which could rapidly adapt to changing situations on the battlefield. I suppose every tank commander wants to be something of a Rommel. All in all, he seemed to me a thorough professional with a marked intellectual bent, but he was not politically ambitious and I could not see him taking it upon himself to force or even encourage any particular political decision. However, he clearly failed to anticipate the fears that his flamboyant style would arouse across the border and there is reason to believe that his political masters were not too pleased with him.

Despite the narrow escape that both countries had from a major disaster, the talks at the Foreign Secretary level were at first little different from any Indo-Pakistan dialogue and had a distinct flavour of mistrust and suspicion. On the Indian side, Alfred Gonsalves, led the delegation. He was not as much as an expert on India-Pakistan relations as his counterpart, Abdul Sattar, and gave the distinct impression of being diffident and indecisive. No doubt this was due to the fact that he was only holding the fort as Acting Foreign Secretary for a short period. Venkateshwaran had left and K.P.S. Menon had not yet returned from China, where he was Ambassador. The first few sessions were hardly auspicious and there was much trading of traditional arguments and counter-arguments. At one stage, our

Foreign Secretary, who had come in a special aircraft, informed Islamabad that he was thinking of returning home because the Indians were being intransigent. He was firmly told by Foreign Minister Sahabzada Yakub Khan not to leave Delhi until an agreement had been reached. In the final event, it was largely due to the flexibility of the military members of both delegations and a last minute intervention by Defence Minister V.P. Singh that what might have been another deadlock was broken.

The two sides agreed to a phased programme of de-escalation. Exercise Brass Tacks was completed without further ado and, a few weeks later, President Zia ul Haq quite dramatically announced that he would visit India to watch a Test Match between the two countries in Jaipur. This 'cricket diplomacy' has often been confused with the actual solution of the Brass Tacks crisis which, in fact, preceded it by several weeks. However, it did go a long way in bringing further sanity, temporary though it might be, to the scene.

President Zia's visit was his third to India during my tenure. Because protocol dictated that it was the turn of India's leader to visit Pakistan, he got around it by calling it an unofficial visit to watch cricket. However, he brought a large delegation and was lodged at Rashtrapati Bhavan, where he spent one night, before going on to stay another night at the Rambagh Palace Hotel in Jaipur. He had a long private session with Rajiv Gandhi at which they decided to set up a direct informal channel between them. Unfortunately, this was never fully used during the remaining time I had in Delhi. The tour was also a public relations success and the President was greeted by large crowds when he visited the shrines of Hazrat Nizamuddin Aulia and Ajmer Sharif. He chatted with the Indian cricketers and received a number of distinguished Indian personalities in his suite at the hotel. When the Rajmata of Jaipur, the legendary Gayatri Devi entered, he welcomed her with the comment: 'Your Highness, thank you for letting me stay in your palace.' Quick as a flash, she replied, 'Not only are you staying in my palace, you are occupying my bedroom.' She was a woman of infinite grace and surpassing beauty and, having spent a lifetime in high society, was by no means slow in repartee. She was followed by Maharaja Bhawani Singh, who was accompanied by a glamorous young lady with a deeply plunging neckline, which seemed to throw the President off-balance every time she leant forward to speak!

The cricket tour by the Pakistan team in 1987, which at one stage seemed threatened by the Brass Tacks crisis, was a great success and our young players found many admirers. Imran Khan was, of course, the main attraction and he led the side to a commendable victory in the series. Both teams were on the best of terms and the crowds, too, were by and large friendly. There were some anxious moments at the end of the one-day match in Hyderabad. Pakistan needed two runs off the last ball to win. Abdul Qadir played it to Azharuddin at deep square leg, completed one run and rashly returned for a second. He was run out by a yard. Had he contented himself with a single, it would have been a tie with Pakistan having the better run-rate. The manager for the Pakistan team unwisely decided to go out on to the field and argue with the umpires that the first run had been validly completed. The crowd began to get restive and the situation could easily have become ugly. Fortunately, Pakistan relented and a public announcement was made that India was the winner. Disappointed but mightily relieved, I returned to my hotel and immediately sent a note of congratulations to Kapil Dev, the Indian Captain.

reflections

My last months in India were relatively uneventful on the professional side but, by then, we had made so many friends that we really did not want to ever leave. I should normally have been moved in 1987 but President Zia had asked Mr Junejo to keep me on, and I received an official letter that I was to stay at least another year.

In the Spring of 1988, President Zia suddenly dismissed Prime Minister Junejo and 'resumed all powers'. Most Indians had never really accepted the claim that I had been making for more than a year that Pakistan was now a full-fledged parliamentary democracy and that the civilian Prime Minister was both de facto and de jure Head of the Government and Chief Executive. I recall trying to make this point to Rajiv Gandhi sitting in his office in the Lok Sabha. He gave a wry smile and said 'Yes, but General Zia still holds the strings.' Thus, the reversion to one-man rule in Pakistan did not cause too much of a stir in India except that there were extensive and, at times, patronizing articles in the Press that real democracy would always remain elusive in Pakistan. Officially, it was almost as if things were reverting to normal after a temporary aberration and the Indians were quite comfortable in, once again, dealing with President Zia ul Haq.

A few weeks later I was ordered to return to Islamabad and take over as Foreign Secretary, which I eventually did in August 1988. This brought to an end an exciting, eventful, thoroughly enjoyable and totally unforgettable stay in India. My opinion that Delhi is the best post for diplomats from Pakistan was reinforced. In all honesty, however, I must admit that, though I had seen some signs of improvement in relations between the two countries and despite the success in averting some crises, towards the end I was overcome with a sense of frustration. At the farewell reception given for me by the diplomatic corps, I felt obliged to say that though I had thoroughly enjoyed my stint, I could not truthfully claim that I was going away satisfied with the job I had done. I do not think any Pakistan envoy to Delhi can make this claim nor, I suspect, can any Indian envoy to Pakistan.

This sense of professional failure was largely offset by the many happy experiences my family and I had at the personal level. We were able to revive many old ties and to forge many new friendships which were to continue after we had left. We received a great deal of affection, the warmest of hospitality and an inordinate measure of understanding. This served to bring home the reality of an unhappy paradox that for more than 50 years, official policies on both sides have run counter to the real wishes of the vast majority of the people. Clearly, they want peace and friendship, but no government in Delhi or Islamabad has been able to ensure this. As Ambassador, this reality always lurked at the back of my mind and destroyed any sense of achievement, leave alone fulfilment.

Diplomats say that the only durable things in their profession are memories. This is true in the sense that they are constantly on the move, friendships are interrupted, environments change and problems vary. As I reflect on my years in Delhi, my memories are, on balance, more positive than negative. Admittedly, the inability to achieve durable results on the professional front still rankles. Subsequent events have proved to be harsh reminders of this failure. On the other hand, living in India and with Indians has, if anything, strengthened my conviction that, some day, both sides will realize where their true interests lie.

Fifteen years on, I still look back to my years in Delhi as the happiest and most interesting of my career. The city itself is rich in history and in culture. It is inhabited by citizens who include the most illustrious names in the arts, the sciences, in business and in public life. It has enchanting gardens and lively bazaars. It also presents modern comforts and pleasures with its hotels and restaurants, its shops, libraries and museums. There was never any difficulty in finding things to do or to keep visitors from Pakistan entertained. They came in hordes, the ladies being particularly interested in shopping for clothes, jewellery and the softest shawls. Indian shopkeepers are among the most courteous and the most professional in the world. They do not hesitate to spread out bolts and bolts of the finest cottons and silks even if you do not buy. They always offer you refreshments and willingly let you take away goods on approval.

For me personally, the greatest pleasure I had in Delhi was from my membership of the Delhi Golf Club. The course is in the very heart of the best residential area. It is of an international standard, with historic monuments dotted all around and peacocks running about on the fairways. Here I could escape from the pressure of work but, at the same time, achieve what I could never do sitting in my office. I was able to mix freely with a wide cross-section of Delhi society, businessmen, civil servants, politicians, military officers, lawyers, journalists, doctors and so on. From all of them, I invariably received nothing but the most gracious friendship. Here also, I was able to establish close personal links with a number of diplomatic colleagues.

The diplomatic corps in India was amongst the most distinguished I have ever worked with. There were over a hundred missions and many of my contemporaries went on to much higher stations in life. Entertainment at the embassies was lavish and it was notable that Indians never shied away from mixing with diplomats. There were very few occasions where the majority of the guests were not locals and they, in turn, entertained foreigners with equal frequency and more than equal style. In this respect, Delhi is far more cosmopolitan than Islamabad, which is a relatively new capital still dominated by bureaucrats. They are wary of being seen in the homes of foreign diplomats, particularly those from certain countries, because it inevitably means that their names get into Intelligence reports. Indians seem to have no such fear. As the Ambassador of Pakistan, I was constantly worried that friends who came to my house regularly and at all hours may be harassed by their Intelligence agencies. I asked some of them and was told that they had indeed been questioned, but had replied that I was their personal or family friend and they had every intention of continuing to meet me. They were never troubled again.

The cost of living in Delhi was, at that time, quite reasonable and I found that my emoluments permitted me to entertain frequently and on a large scale. There were times when I had up to 200 guests at a party. The catering facilities were excellent, and we were often able to entertain outdoors with stalls set up in the garden, with each offering a different delicacy. Our National Day reception was held on the vast lawns of the chancery and the whole building was brilliantly illuminated. The number of guests was, on an average, more than 1500.

India as a country was, even for someone who belonged to the region, full of fascination. The varied natural beauty of the countryside, the historical richness, and the different sub-cultures all made travelling a pleasure. Facilities for visitors are second to none and Indians are quite used to foreigners and do not treat them as objects of curiosity.

Having said so many nice things about India and the Indians, I continue to agonize, like many others, over the wide diversity, indeed the stark contradiction, which prevails between the attitudes of the people and the actions of their government. I am sure Indians find the same dichotomy in Pakistan.

Can this, I wonder, be traced back to the experience of 50 years or perhaps the history of more than a thousand years? Is it due to the horrors of Partition? Is it because of a basic and unbridgeable difference in the characteristics and ambitions of their ruling classes or can it be ascribed to a genuine clash between the interests of the two countries? The answer is by no means clear and, no doubt, the causes are multiple. I do not for a moment imagine that when it was decided to divide British India into two separate and independent states, any of those concerned wished for or foresaw that they would become implacable foes. Rather, the hope was that with the largest and very substantial minority community having its own homeland, communal strife would be prevented and the two neighbours would exploit their commonalities and their proximity to the greatest mutual advantage. The Founder of Pakistan, Mohammed Ali Jinnah, himself expressed this hope and, even after Partition, spoke of going back regularly to his home in Bombay (now Mumbai). Unfortunately, at that time, the Congress leadership kept harping on the theme that the separation was temporary and a united India would soon re-emerge. In the months immediately following Independence, their actions were clearly designed to undermine and weaken the infant state. Added to this was the violent hatred generated by the massacres that took place in the summer of 1947, leaving so many families bereaved, homeless and destitute. Then came the Kashmir dispute. All these factors naturally made the fledgling state of Pakistan extremely anxious about its security and, given the imbalance in size and in resources, it began to look for allies and friends so that it would be less vulnerable. It found a ready and effective partner in the United States, which was committed to the concept of containing communism through a network of military alliances. So, in the 1950s, Pakistan entered into the Baghdad Pact (later CENTO) and the South East Asia Treaty Organization (SEATO) and began to receive massive military assistance. Pakistan's partners in these alliances never intended them to be directed against India. They recognized that India, as the largest country in the region, the biggest non-communist state, and the best example of democracy in the Third World would always be more important to them. Yet Pakistan, through its own interpretation of these alliances, drew a certain sense of security from them.

In retrospect, it seems debatable whether India's strong reaction to America's friendship with Pakistan was the wisest under the circumstances. To say it was justified because Nehru wanted to keep the Cold War out of the subcontinent or that he feared a militarily strong Pakistan is hardly convincing. When it came to the national interest, India itself turned to the West for arms during and after the short conflict with China in 1962. Nor did it hesitate to align itself with the Soviet Union when this was advantageous. Had the Indians shown greater understanding of the fears of a smaller neighbour and taken the option of further allaying those fears, early foundations for a stable relationship could have been laid. Instead, the Indian reaction was sharp and hostile. Pakistan's alliance with the West was used as a somewhat tenuous argument for reneging on the commitment to honour the wishes of the people of Kashmir, expressed through a free and impartial plebiscite, and India began to lean towards the Soviet Union, thus further encouraging a role for the superpowers in South Asia. In return, it received massive economic and military assistance in addition to the benefits of a Soviet veto in its favour in Indo-Pakistan disputes before the United Nations.

As the years passed, the new state of Pakistan began to find its feet, to make more friends and to develop economically. Moreover, its geo-strategic location made it an important country on the world stage and talk of its re-absorption into India abated. Unfortunately, however, two big mistakes were made. First, the war of 1965 lent some credence to the charge that American military assistance had emboldened Pakistan to the point of risking an open conflict with its larger neighbour. Second, the alienation of East Pakistan reached a point in 1971 when ruthless military suppression was deemed to be the only way to preserve the integrity of the country. The Indian intervention in East Pakistan and its role in the creation of Bangladesh revived fears that the Indian aim of undoing Pakistan remained unchanged. Moreover, this time there was an added dimension. The Pakistan army was humiliated and this left deep scars on it soul. Defeated though it was, this same army was soon to re-emerge as the most powerful force in domestic politics and the arbiter on crucial issues, particularly relations with India. It harboured a deep-seated distrust of its neighbour and the outlook of its officers and soldiers was to be continuingly moulded along these lines.

By the time I went to India in 1984, Bangladesh had remained a separate and independent state for more than a decade and the idea of reabsorbing Pakistan into a united India had few buyers among the Indian intelligentsia. Indeed, I found many Indians speaking of a stable and prosperous Pakistan as being in their own interest. I remember Rajiv Gandhi himself telling me in private that he considered the Soviet military intervention in Afghanistan as much of a threat to India as it was to Pakistan. This was a far cry from Mrs Gandhi's soft reaction to Moscow's adventure.

Also, at that time, I noticed that Indian priorities were shifting. The preoccupation with regional domination was giving way to a larger ambition of being a principal actor on the world stage. With the demise of the Soviet Union and the new emphasis on democracy and free markets, India – with an impressive industrial and technological base, with a large, educated middle class and with one of the largest consumer potentials in the world – began to see itself as a member of the big league. To be seen as such by others, it could not afford the reputation of a regional bully, trying to subjugate its smaller neighbours and constantly quarrelling with them. It became more important for it to build an image of a dynamic economy and a modern, technologically advancing country. No less important was the image of a stable democracy with respect for the rule of law and for human freedoms. This new outlook, as I see it, crystallized in the 90s when democracy and free enterprise were ascendant throughout the world. During this period, India developed a rare consensus on economic policies and its domestic politics entered an era of coalitions, where agreement on extreme positions became more and more difficult to achieve. Instead, a national commitment to becoming a power with a world vision, ready to compete economically, militarily powerful in its own right and yet able to earn the trust and confidence of its smaller neighbours became the overriding objective. India, one might say, had decided to graduate from 'bigness' to 'greatness'. The destruction of Pakistan did not fit into this scheme of things. Unfortunately, however, there remained a certain small-mindeness and a penchant for sophistry which, unless discarded, will always prevent India from acquiring the true personality of a great power. These together with the rise of the communal Hindu sentiment in its internal politics, are likely to be the major obstacles in the way of its global ambitions. The rise of Hindu extremism will inevitably damage its image as a secular democracy and also hinder the chances of improving relations with its neighbours.

My view that India has moved away from its earlier preoccupation with regional domination does not appeal to the most powerful elements in Pakistan. They still believe that India's primary aim is the undoing of Pakistan. Some also think there are domestic political advantages and benefits to be gained from propagating this belief. Many, however, have now moved away from a fear of re-absorption to one of hegemony. India, they concede, may not want to absorb Pakistan with all its problems, but it does want to dominate the region and reduce all other countries to the status of vassals. Resistance to this ambition is considered a matter of national honour and such resistance, it is argued, can only be possible if Pakistan remains militarily strong. As I see it, this attitude reflects not strong resolve as much as a basic lack of confidence in the country's permanent place in the community of nations. Secondly, it implies that, if peace and friendship are attained, Pakistan does not have the economic, political, social and cultural ability to withstand Indian hegemony. I do not believe that either of these fears is well-founded. Pakistan has now become an important member of the world community and cannot be wished away that easily. Its physical security does not hang by the slender thread of its nuclear deterrent alone, as some proclaim. If it does not invite aggression by its own provocative actions and policies, there appears little reason for any country to want to destroy it. The external dangers to its existence are too often exaggerated. On the fear of hegemony, I am convinced that, given the opportunity and the right leadership, the people of Pakistan have the talent, the skills and the ability to compete with anyone. I would even go as far as to say that, with problems of a much smaller scale than India faces, Pakistan could forge ahead in many fields.

All this is, of course, dependent entirely on Pakistan finding a durable internal equilibrium. As long as all the strands of the national fabric are not pulled together to form a cohesive pattern and unless national security is seen as a composite of economic, social, political and moral strength, the sense of physical insecurity will continue to prevail. The way will remain open for it to be exploited by vested interests and the bogey of external threats will be used to divert attention from the failures of those in power. It has now been 56 years and the country has yet to find answers to basic political issues like the form of government, the role of the army, the structures of governance and the relationship between the Centre and the federating units. On the economic front, lack of continuity in policies, corruption in the highest places and decisions taken on personal whims have resulted in an increasing percentage of the population living below the poverty line as each year passes. Foreign investment has become virtually non-existent and the cost of living is constantly rising. In the midst of all this, the ruling classes continue to live in great luxury and the mood of the nation constantly wavers between rage and despair. At some stage, the priority to be given to domestic issues will have to be recognized, and this can only come about if, on the external front, postures are adopted which will make these issues easier and not more difficult to resolve. In the tense environment that prevails all over the globe today, it is imperative for Pakistan's ruling elite to understand that adventurous and high-risk policies could well invite the very disasters that it believes it is preventing.

It is strange that so little importance has been given to the enormous gains which will accrue to both countries if they cooperate with each other. Together, they would be a powerful economic and political force in the international arena. Certainly, their resources could be put to much better use for the benefit of their peoples. On the other hand, nothing is to be gained by living in a state of perpetual hostility. For more than a year, they have not even been talking to each other. This is a sad reflection on the wisdom of their leaders.

In the winter of 2001, India took some extreme measures to signify its exasperation with what it terms 'cross-border terrorism'. These were triggered by a terrorist attack on the Indian Parliament in December 2001. Islamabad roundly condemned the incident and, certainly, there has been no evidence to date that Pakistan was, in any way, involved. The amassing of troops on the border, the recall of the High Commissioner, the subsequent expulsion of his counterpart and the breaking off of travel links were steps that plunged the sub-continent into a state of deep uncertainty. I, for one, found it difficult to understand this violent reaction by India.

Fortunately, there have been some positive developments of late, which reinforce my conviction that Mr Vajpayee is essentially a man of peace. Earlier this year, he initiated, once more, a revival of the normalization process by deciding to restore full diplomatic representation and some travel links. Pakistan responded not just positively, but with enthusiasm. Mr Vajpayee has termed this his last attempt to establish a durable relationship of peace and amity with Pakistan. We can only hope that it will succeed and the forces in both countries which have, in the past, frustrated all such attempts, will have learnt their lesson and will respect the wishes of the people. As I write these words, however, the resumption of a full and

unconditional dialogue remains in some doubt. Does this mean
that the initiative will prove to be another false start? We must
all hope and pray that it will not. The consequences of another
failure will be disastrous. A break with the past has to be made.
It is not a time for suspicion and cynicism. Nor is it a time for
euphoria. It is a time for the recognition of realities. It is time for
India and Pakistan to be at peace.

memories of pakistan

g parthasarathy

the year 1998 was, in many ways, a memorable year in my life. I was scheduled to retire from the Indian Foreign Service, as High Commissioner in Australia, on 31 May. My wife, Shanti, and I had packed our baggage and were planning to return to our home in Delhi, after visiting our younger daughter, Priya, in San Jose, California, immediately after my retirement. We had just spent a wonderful weekend with friends in the Indian community in Sydney and were getting set to return to Canberra by road on the morning of 12 May, when I asked our hosts, Vikram and Mala Mehta, to switch on the television to listen to the BBC news broadcast. The headlines were that the Indian Prime Minister, Atal Bihari Vajpayee, had announced that India had carried out three nuclear tests, including one of a thermonuclear weapon, the previous day.

I knew that, given the strong sentiments that had been voiced in Australia after the nuclear tests that France and China had conducted in earlier years, all hell would break loose in Canberra. I was pretty certain that in my absence Deputy High Commissioner Brij Tyagi would be summoned and given a long homily about nuclear non-proliferation by Foreign Minister

Alexander Downer, who would pose as a champion of nuclear non-proliferation in Parliament and the media. I was determined that this should not happen. I told Tyagi that if he was summoned by the Foreign Office he should not go. He should insist that on such an important issue only the High Commissioner would see the Australian Foreign Minister. Despite depending on America's nuclear umbrella for their own security, the Australians seemed to believe that they could lecture and sermonize to others on the virtues of nuclear abstinence. Along with some other countries like Canada and Holland (derisively known in New Delhi as the 'New Evangelists') they remained members of military alliances that based their defence strategies on the nuclear arsenal of countries like the USA, UK, and France. Yet they sought to be crusaders in disarming the unarmed through unequal treaties like the nuclear Non-Proliferation Treaty (NPT) or the Comprehensive Test Ban Treaty.

I was determined that Australian hypocrisy on nuclear issues should not go unchallenged. I told Downer and the Australian media in no uncertain terms that if Australians could base their security on the nuclear deterrence of others, India had every right to make its own choices and develop its own nuclear deterrent. In an interview with ABC's prime time anchorwoman, Maxine Mckew, I noted that in the 1950s and 1960s Australia had permitted the UK to carry out scores of atmospheric nuclear tests on its soil. The resulting radioactivity had played havoc with the lives of aborigines. In these circumstances, it was rather odd for Australians to shed tears over possible radioactivity from our underground nuclear tests. Refusing to get drawn into any controversy over Pakistan's nuclear tests, I said that Pakistan had every right to test nuclear weapons if it felt that such weapons were necessary for its security. I also noted that Pakistan's nuclear programme had commenced in 1972, well before we carried out our first nuclear test in 1974. While these arguments were well received by people in Australia, the rather immature Foreign Minister, Alexander Downer, somehow felt that India would be cowed down by his aggressive posturing.

Pakistan's High Commissioner in Australia, Qamar Zaman, was a mild-mannered police official, who had been sent to Australia by Prime Minister Nawaz Sharif as a reward for his having acted tough in prosecuting Benazir Bhutto and her husband Asif Zardari on allegations of corruption. I was really shocked at the way the Pakistanis stomached Australian insults, including the peremptory expulsion of a high-level Parliamentary delegation led by the Chairman of their Senate, Wasim Sajjad, that was visiting Australia at the invitation of their counterparts. The Indian community in Australia was very nervous about the adverse reaction they would be subjected to following our nuclear tests. Our media blitz did, however, succeed in persuading Australian public opinion that their Government's policies were marked by double standards. Australians can be very fair-minded. New Delhi acted tough in response to Australian actions. Meaningless Australian sanctions were answered in kind. For once, I was satisfied that New Delhi had decided that diplomatic niceties would not come in the way of responding strongly to those who chose to be sanctimonious and have high moral pretensions on issues of nuclear policy, even as they were members of military alliances that sanctified the possession and use of nuclear weapons.

Despite the hostility of the Australian Government and political establishment towards our nuclear tests, the reaction of ordinary people and the Australian media and academic community to our nuclear tests was marked by remarkable candour and openness. I was given free access to voice our viewpoints to television, the newspapers and at academic institutions. Even environmentalist groups appreciated our assertion that rather than hide under an American nuclear umbrella, Australia should be working with countries like India to promote universal nuclear disarmament. Given their passion for sports, Australians play tough, but fair. Just when things seemed to be settling down, Shanti and I left the quiet and serene surroundings of Canberra to move into a totally new environment in Islamabad.

We were in Delhi for the wedding of our daughter Rukmini, when Foreign Secretary Krishnan Raghunath informed me that I had to return as soon as possible to Canberra and leave immediately thereafter for Islamabad. This came as no surprise, as I had been told a few months earlier that the Prime Minister, Atal Bihari Vajpayee, acting on the advice of his National Security Adviser Brajesh Misra had approved my posting to Islamabad. Misra had been a career diplomat who had held key assignments in China and New York. His father D.P. Misra, who was Chief Minister of the state of Madhya Pradesh, was a close associate of Prime Minister Indira Gandhi. Brajesh Misra's career suffered when differences arose between his father and Mrs Gandhi. After returning to Delhi from a high-level UN assignment in New York, Misra joined the opposition Bharatiya Janata Party (BJP) and became the head of its foreign policy set up. His balanced views on foreign policy matters made him a close confidant of Party President Atal Bihari Vajpayee. It was really Misra who ensured that India successfully exercised its nuclear option within weeks of Vajpayee taking charge as Prime Minister. Misra was also primarily responsible for the firm, confident and determined manner in which India faced the economic and technological sanctions and negotiated with several key interlocutors after the nuclear tests. While his dual role as the Prime Minister's Principal Secretary and National Security Adviser became controversial with the passage of time, there is little doubt that he deserves substantial credit for the firm and sophisticated manner in which the post-nuclear tests scenario was handled.

A second stint in Pakistan was something that Shanti and I looked forward to with mixed feelings. We had spent three and a half memorable and pleasant years in Karachi from January

1982 to July 1985. Those were interesting and relatively tension-free years in our relations with Pakistan. Karachi was a booming metropolitan city. Its population was dominated by Urdu-speaking *muhajirs* (*muhajir* is the Urdu word for refugee) who had migrated to Pakistan from Muslim minority provinces and princely states in India. The *muhajirs* played a key role in Pakistan's national life in the early years after Pakistan emerged as an independent country. The new nation's founding father, Mohammed Ali Jinnah, and its first Prime Minister, Liaquat Ali Khan, were *muhajirs*, whose ancestral homes were in India. But one of the great ironies of the newly independent state of Pakistan was that its founding fathers were not natives of their new homeland, but people from a neighbouring country who felt that they would have a better future in their new homeland, where they would be part of a religious majority. The *muhajirs* had never bargained for the fact that with time they would have to give way to the dominance of the indigenous people of Pakistan—Sindhis, Baluchis, Seraikis, Punjabis and Pashtuns, who would consistently regard them as 'outsiders' in their new homeland. Maulana Abdul Kalam Azad, who was one of the foremost leaders in India's struggle against colonial domination, had warned the *Muhajirs* that they would soon find themselves regarded as foreign intruders and outsiders by the local people, if they chose to leave their native land and migrate to new surroundings.

While the *muhajirs* had played an important role in Pakistan in its early years, the centre of political and economic power inevitably shifted to Punjab when the army started dominating the country's national life. Their national role and importance declined with time. This trend became even more pronounced when Bangladesh became an independent country in 1971 and a Sindhi leader, Zulfiqar Ali Bhutto, became the country's President, with his cousin Mumtaz Bhutto becoming the Chief Minister of Sind. Even within the Sind province, the *muhajirs* had to face manifestations of Sindhi assertiveness on issues like the official language of the Province in which they lived. As time passed, there was also a feeling of nostalgia for their ancestral homes. There was a desire to revive familial ties with their kith and kin in India. The Hindi film industry had fired their imagination. The message of the Hindi films, which extolled secular values and communal harmony, and in which Muslim actors and singers played a major role, contradicted the vituperative outpourings against India and the alleged discrimination against Muslims in India in mass circulation Urdu newspapers like the *Jang* and the *Nawai Waqt*. Gujarati-speaking *muhajirs* and even those who were Urdu speaking often sought marital partners for their sons and daughters from their kinsmen in India.

from simla to agra

When India and Pakistan resumed diplomatic relations in 1975, after the 1971 Bangladesh conflict, it was agreed that India would re-open its Consulate General in Karachi. Pakistan, in turn, would establish a Consulate General in Bombay (now Mumbai). That these two consulates were to be established in the industrial and business hubs of the two countries indicated that their staffs would not only facilitate people-to-people contacts, but also lay the basis for a strong economic and business relationship. New Delhi was particularly keen that past hostilities should be subsumed in wide-ranging cooperation and increasing human interaction. Prime Minister Indira Gandhi had taken the assurances given by Zulfiqar Ali Bhutto when they met in Simla in July 1972 at face value and presumed that as the climate of relations improved, an atmosphere would be created in which the vexed Kashmir issue could be resolved, by formalizing the status quo.

Professor P.N. Dhar, who was then Mrs Gandhi's Secretary and a member of the Indian negotiating team in Simla, told me many years later that Mrs Gandhi had been persuaded by

Bhutto in Simla that while he was not then in a position to move towards a settlement of the Kashmir issue on the basis of accepting the Line of Control as an International Border in 1972, he would nevertheless move in that direction in course of time. It still astonishes many of us who knew Mrs Gandhi to be, in Henry Kissinger's words, 'a cold-blooded practitioner of realpolitik,' that she went wrong in her assessment of Zulfiqar Ali Bhutto. P.N. Haksar, who led the Indian negotiating team in Simla, was to remark just before he died that if there was one action that he regretted, it was the advice he gave to Mrs Gandhi in Simla that she should not allow a situation to be created where Bhutto was compelled to return home empty-handed from the Simla Summit. We, however, never seem to learn from history. It was precisely such wishful thinking that led to Prime Minister Atal Bihari Vajpayee facing a media and diplomatic disaster during his Agra Summit with General Pervez Musharraf in 2001.

As I look back on the many years that I spent in dealing with Pakistan-related issues in New Delhi, Islamabad and elsewhere in capitals like Moscow and Washington, I cannot help asserting that amongst India's leaders, it was Indira Gandhi who perhaps best understood how to balance the security, international and internal political dimensions of our relations with Pakistan. Why then did she go wrong in assessing Bhutto in Simla in July 1972? One important factor behind her thinking was the advice of her leftist advisers like P.N. Haksar, who argued that India should not seek to impose a Treaty of Versailles on a defeated and demoralized Pakistan, as this would revive militaristic thinking in that country. This is an argument that the Americans invariably use when asking India to 'engage' Pakistan in order to bail out one or another military dictator who happens to be their favourite at any given point in time. Indian negotiators believed that as Bhutto was under tremendous pressure to secure the release of 93,000 Pakistan prisoners held by India, he would respond to their early release by seeking to accommodate Indian concerns on other issues. This was yet another instance of Indian inability to comprehend the Pakistani mind.

Bhutto knew that international pressure would compel India, sooner rather than later, to release the Pakistani prisoners. What he urgently wanted to get back was the nearly 12,000 square kilometres of Pakistani territory that was in Indian hands at the end of the 1971 conflict. The main failing in our negotiating strategy in Simla flowed from the fact that we did not understand that Bhutto's priority was the return of territories captured by us during the conflict and not the return of prisoners of war. We thus failed to use the return of territory as an effective bargaining chip. 'Land for Peace' is an argument we should have firmly used in negotiating with Pakistan after the 1971 conflict.

It was the inability of Indian negotiators to understand Bhutto's priorities that led to their playing into his hands in Simla. Bhutto's arguments that he was just not in a position to agree to a Kashmir settlement on the basis of the status quo and that he would require time to bring his countrymen around to agreeing to this were too easily accepted at face value. Further, rather than linking Indian withdrawals from territories across the international border captured in 1971 to implementation of the assurances that Bhutto gave on Kashmir, our negotiators gave back the land captured during the 1971 conflict unconditionally. They seemed to have forgotten the cardinal principle that post-dated cheques have no value in international affairs, especially when they are signed by persons who had sworn to wage a thousand-year war against India only a few years earlier. But what is perhaps not so well known is that after assuming power Bhutto had taken two vital decisions. The first decision that he took was in January 1972 to acquire the capabilities, at any cost, for Pakistan to develop a nuclear deterrent to counter India's conventional superiority. The second decision was to develop a more balanced relationship with the two superpowers and build bridges to the Soviet Union. This was supplemented by strong leftist rhetoric about a commitment to 'Islamic Socialism', while developing close ties with radical Arab States like Libya and Syria.

Bhutto visited Moscow in April 1972 and appears to have held out assurances to the Soviet leadership that he would withdraw from western military pacts like CENTO and SEATO. It was implicitly made clear to the Soviet leadership that in return he expected them to lean on India to withdraw from occupied territories and release prisoners of war immediately. Around the same time, Bhutto sent hints to the Soviet leadership that their understanding would enable him to move towards concluding a treaty with the Soviet Union, similar to the Indo-Soviet Treaty of August 1971. His efforts met with immediate success. The Soviet leadership let India know that they expected us to move purposefully towards resolving issues like the return of prisoners and normalizing relations with Pakistan expeditiously. (Exchanges between Bhutto and the Soviet Union on a Pakistan-Soviet Friendship Treaty continued till Bhutto was overthrown in a military coup staged by General Zia ul Haq in July 1977.) A visibly concerned Sardar Swaran Singh, who was then the Foreign Minister, accompanied by Foreign Secretary T.N. Kaul, arrived in Moscow for talks with the Soviet leadership in May 1972. (I was posted in Moscow as First Secretary (Political) at that time.) Given President Nixon's now famous tilt against India, Indira Gandhi obviously did not want to be perceived as being insensitive to Soviet concerns. This was particularly important, as she was averse to endorsing the Brezhnev Doctrine on Collective Security in Asia. She was also determined to see that the Soviet Union did not assume a role like it did earlier in determining the course of Indo-Pakistan relations, as Prime Minister Kosygin had succeeded in doing in Tashkent in 1966. (The Tashkent Agreement was followed by the commencement of a Soviet-Pakistan military relationship.) Any failure to reach an agreement in Simla would have led to complications in India's entire foreign policy posture, with Soviet pressure mounting for a mediatory role.

While it could be claimed that India conceded too much in Simla, it would be necessary to analyze the then prevailing international environment to understand why it was important for Mrs Gandhi to reach an agreement with Bhutto and not allow the Simla Summit to fail. The Simla Agreement did give us a number of gains. It provided a viable and realistic framework for the progressive normalization of relations with Pakistan, through the re-establishment of diplomatic relations, the promotion of people-to-people contacts, the development of trade, economic and cultural ties and the resolution of outstanding issues, including the issue of Jammu and Kashmir. More importantly, the Agreement made specific reference to the settlement of all differences through peaceful and bilateral means. The past UN Resolutions on Jammu and Kashmir were made even more redundant and irrelevant when India refused to undertake any withdrawals from areas in Jammu and Kashmir captured in 1971, leading to the replacement of the UN-mandated Ceasefire Line in Jammu and Kashmir by a new bilaterally negotiated Line of Control. The Agreement also provided for both sides respecting the inviolability of this Line of Control. When Nawaz Sharif's Ambassador to Washington, Riaz Khokkar, tried to pretend to the State Department during the Kargil conflict of 1999 that the Line of Control had not been clearly marked and delineated, he was bluntly told that the United States had details of the maps signed by senior military commanders of India and Pakistan delineating the Line of Control and that Pakistan had to respect the sanctity of this line and end its intrusion in the Kargil sector.

The Simla Agreement remains the best available framework for normalizing relations with Pakistan. Hawks in the Pakistan establishment like former Foreign Minister Abdul Sattar have invariably labelled the Simla Agreement as an unequal agreement, a 'diktat' imposed on a nation defeated in war. Sattar and others like him have consistently sought to sideline and undermine the importance of this agreement. During the Agra Summit in 2001, the astute and experienced Sattar outmanoeuvred the Indian negotiators led by their inexperienced Foreign Minister, Jaswant Singh. India came perilously close to signing a declaration that would have not made any mention of the Simla Agreement and the Lahore Declaration. What was particularly surprising about our approach to the Agra Summit was our unseemly haste in agreeing to develop an entirely new framework for bilateral relations with Pakistan, while omitting all reference to past agreements like the Simla Agreement and the Lahore Declaration, that had been concluded with democratically elected Governments in Pakistan. Mercifully, better sense ultimately prevailed in Agra and we realized that no useful purpose would be served by pandering to the Kashmir-centric obsessions of General Musharraf. There is a tendency in the Indian media and amongst sections of our intelligentsia to suggest that with time we should be 'flexible' and forget the past and seek new and innovative approaches and frameworks to our relations with Pakistan. While such sentiments are unexceptionable, they betray a total ignorance of the complex nature of our relations with our western neighbour.

An Israeli friend of mine once discussed our negotiating tactics at Simla and Agra with me at some length. He told me that Indians seem to lack realism when negotiating with adversaries. He recalled his own participation in negotiations with Egypt. He said that before entering into negotiations, the Israeli negotiators were given a clear brief about what incremental progress was expected in each round of negotiations. It is always necessary to speak from a position of strength and not let your adversary get a feeling that you would be upset if negotiations fail: this was the mature advice of this Israeli negotiator. Finally, the adversary should have no illusions about what your bottom line is. Summit meetings without proper preparations are recipes for disaster, especially if you are dealing with a ruler like General Musharraf who has deep-set prejudices and makes no secret of his abiding animosity towards India. One sincerely hopes that when India and Pakistan do resume talks, we enter into a negotiating process that is carefully structured, with a clear understanding on both sides that the process is going to be time consuming and requiring patience.

pakistan under zia

While my second tenure in Pakistan was in Islamabad, it was really my first stay in Pakistan as Consul General in Karachi that led to the establishment of many lasting friendships with Pakistanis whom Shanti, our two daughters and I got to meet. These are friendships that we cherish—with people who showed so much understanding, consideration and indeed affection. We reached Karachi from Washington in December 1981. We moved into the palatial residence of the Consul General located just next to the residence of Zulfiqar Ali Bhutto in the best residential area of Clifton in Karachi. The Indian Government had purchased this residence in 1948 for the Indian High Commissioner. Its original owners were a most gracious and charming Parsi couple, the Sopariwallas. Sopariwalla recalled to us how Pakistan's first Prime Minister Liaquat Ali Khan had persuaded him to sell the house to the Indian High Commission after Liaqat had been asked personally by Jawaharlal Nehru to help out his envoy in securing a suitable residence. Nehru took an active interest in seeing that India's envoys abroad lived and conducted themselves in a manner that did credit to the country they represented. New Delhi has, by and large, been farsighted in acquiring properties for its representatives abroad to live in an appropriate and befitting manner. The only problem one faces now with accommodation constructed by us is that the norms prescribed for the size of residential accommodation make the apartments we construct just too small for appropriate entertainment by Embassy officials.

The Clifton residence of the Indian Consul General in Karachi was far more spacious and majestic than the Indian High Commissioner's residence in Islamabad. The passage of time has unfortunately seen a marked change in attitudes and approaches to the relationship. In 1948, the Pakistani Prime Minister, Liaqat Ali Khan, personally intervened to ensure that the Indian envoy was helped in securing residential accommodation. During the Lahore Summit in February 1999, I drew Prime Minister Nawaz Sharif's attention to the fact that we had paid for and been allotted land for the High Commissioner's residence in Islamabad almost two decades ago. Despite this, the Government of Pakistan had not handed over the allotted land to us. Nawaz Sharif did act on this matter and we did receive a communication asking us to take over the land. But his Foreign Secretary, Shamshad Ahmad, and Additional Secretary, Tariq Altaf, just refused to take any follow up action on the matter and undermined this entire gesture, made at the highest level by Prime Minister Nawaz Sharif. It is precisely such behaviour by officials in the Pakistan Foreign Office and in their Intelligence establishment that results in almost every Indian diplomat posted in Pakistan viewing the Pakistani establishment with suspicion, if not hostility.

After Benazir Bhutto's Government closed the Indian Consulate General in Karachi in 1993, the Pakistan Government made every effort to see that we were not allowed to properly maintain the properties owned by us in that city. Efforts by us to get a security agency to look after our properties were constantly thwarted by the Pakistan Foreign Office and Intelligence agencies. This was naturally a matter of concern to us. Shanti and I were shocked to see how our properties in Karachi, including our beautiful residence, were vandalized after we closed our consulate. We did, after all, retain very fond memories of the days we spent with our children in Clifton. I asked Benazir, who was then voicing firm support for better relations with India, why she chose to order the closure of our Consulate in Karachi when Shanti and I met her in March 1999 in her new residence, 'Bilawal House'. She had earlier been forced to vacate the ancestral Bhutto residence located just adjacent to the Indian Consul General's residence in the plush Clifton area of Karachi, by her estranged sister-in-law, Ghinwa Bhutto. She claimed that anti-India sentiments had grown strong after the destruction of the Babri Masjid in Ayodhya in December 1992. But Benazir knew better than anyone else that the ISI regarded our presence in Karachi with great suspicion. The *muhajirs* of Sind often used to point out that their Punjabi-dominated Government was totally unsympathetic to their requests to facilitate their travel to India and to make it easy for their relatives in India to visit them. In marked contrast, India adopted very liberal norms in facilitating such people-to-people contacts. The Babri Mosque demolition provided a convenient pretext for the ISI to secure the closure of our Consulate.

General Zia ul Haq was Pakistan's supreme ruler in the early 1980s. The Punjabi-dominated army called the shots in every sphere of national life. Senior Lieutenant Generals appointed as Governors ruled Pakistan's four provinces and the writ of martial law courts in prosecuting anyone who challenged the hegemony of military rule was supreme. While their Indian counterparts at best owned scooters or motorcycles and could not think of building an apartment till they were relatively senior in service, it was a common sight to see Majors and Lieutenant Colonels of the Pakistan Army driving their own cars and owning their own houses in the plush localities of Lahore, Karachi and Islamabad. Pakistan, then in the grips of a military dictatorship, had become the torchbearer and 'frontline state' of the 'free world' because of its role as the conduit for arms and financial assistance to fundamentalist Afghan mujahideen in the jihad against what President Reagan described as the 'evil empire'. Determined to quell all opposition from the Pakistan People's Party (PPP) and other democratic forces, Zia adopted a two-pronged strategy. He jailed important leaders like Benazir Bhutto. He simultaneously attempted to prop up his own favourites like Nawaz Sharif in a newly formed faction of the Muslim League. Fundamentalist parties like the Jamaat-i-Islami were armed and assisted in establishing links with their counterparts involved in the Afghanistan jihad. Thus armed, the fundamentalist organizations were used by the Army's Inter Services Intelligence (ISI) to intimidate and even eliminate opposition activists, including students.

Lacking a viable domestic political platform or economic programme, General Zia embarked on what he claimed was a programme of progressive Islamization of the country. He held that Islamic principles embodied in the Shariat would be the basis of governance in the country. Claiming that mainstream political parties had ruined the country, he embarked on a policy of what he called 'de-politicization' of the country. Zia had a capacity to play to many audiences. Needing the financial support of Saudi Arabia, he regularly visited Mecca to display his Wahabi credentials and keep his links with Wahabi elements in parties like the Jamaat-i-Islami. At the same time, he recognized that the bulk of his countrymen were wedded to the practices of Sufi Islam. This constituency was kept happy by visits to Sufi shrines like those in Ajmer in India. But even as he resorted to such gimmicks to promote Islamization in Pakistan, Zia was laying the seeds for future sectarian conflict by the policies he adopted in supporting Sunni fundamentalist groups fighting Soviet occupation in Afghanistan. Alarmed by the growth of Saudi Arabian-backed armed groups in Pakistan and by attacks on Shia shrines and processions, Iran responded by lending support to militant Shia groups. The groups that started arming themselves during his rule were to later indulge in armed clashes and bloodletting, and to tear Pakistani society apart on religious-sectarian lines. If an American-backed Ayub Khan adopted policies that led to the breakup of the country on linguistic lines, future generations in Pakistan will undoubtedly hold the American-backed Zia ul Haq responsible for the promotion of the 'AK 47 Gun Culture' in his country.

While earlier military rulers like Ayub and Yahya Khan did not hesitate to resort to bluff, bluster and brinkmanship to deal with India, Zia was far shrewder in his approach. (Mr Vajpayee and his colleagues should consider themselves fortunate that rather than having to deal with a shrewd and indeed cunning operator like General Zia, they have to deal with General Musharraf, who is given to shooting from the hip!) Recognizing that a direct confrontation with India would be disastrous, Zia chose to adopt a strategy of resorting to 'low intensity conflict'. He had successfully persuaded Prime Minister Morarji Desai that he wanted peace and reconciliation with India. But Indira Gandhi was an altogether different kettle of fish. His first meeting with her at the Commonwealth Summit in Harare in 1980 was a disaster. Indira Gandhi was a shrewd judge of people and she felt from the very outset that there was something phony about Zia ul Haq's profession of good intentions. It did not take long for her to be proved right. Even as he spoke to Indian visitors with seeming humility and charm, Zia was assiduously stoking sentiments of separatism in Punjab in India. Sikh pilgrims visiting their holy shrines in Pakistan were sought to be subverted and a massive infrastructure created for promoting Sikh separatism.

Despite the political challenges, life in Karachi in the 1980s was most pleasant. My predecessor, Mani Shankar Aiyer, had done a really good job in befriending a wide cross section of people in Karachi. The Indian Consul General was widely sought after, primarily because virtually everyone in Karachi wanted to visit India to meet friends and relatives. While it was the declared policy of the Government of India to have a liberal visa regime to encourage people-to-people contact, in actual fact the Home Ministry had placed absurd restrictions on the issue of visas. These restrictions, in effect, rendered the stated policy of the Government quite meaningless. While Mani and I have continued to differ on many aspects of our relations with Pakistan for over two decades now, both of us were agreed that we would ignore many of our Home Ministry's diktats. We both chose to go by the letter and spirit of the Government's policies and were liberal in issuing visas to those choosing to visit India. We issued nearly 250,000 visas annually to enable Pakistanis to visit India. I attached the highest importance to this vital function of the Consulate General. I made it a point to visit the visa section everyday to ensure that the intending visitors faced no problems in getting visas and relaxed in comfort while waiting to apply for visas.

The visa section in our Consulate worked in a unique manner. The strength of our staff was such that they could issue only around 350 visas per day. But the demand for visas invariably exceeded this figure. We had, however, told our Pakistani friends that in order to avoid any inconvenience to them we would issue visas the same day that they applied. The problem was resolved by getting the wives of officials to work in the visa section to process visa applications. We also made it a point to open separate counters for women and provide applicants with toilets, cold drinking water and fans while they waited for their visas. These measures did not go unnoticed by ordinary Pakistanis. They found that while Indian officials treated them with politeness and consideration, the local police harassed them, even as they stood in queues waiting to enter the Indian consulate premises. I do believe that among the factors that contributed to the alienation of the *muhajir* community in Karachi was the fact that while their relatives were harassed, delayed and humiliated while applying for visas at the Punjabi-dominated Pakistan High Commission in Delhi, the Indian Mission in Karachi treated them with dignity, courtesy and consideration. The ISI saw the Indian Consulate General in Karachi as a virtual thorn in their flesh. The tragic demolition of the Babri Masjid in Ayodhya in 1992, that badly dented India's image as a uniquely secular and plural country, inevitably led to a rise in anti-Indian sentiments in Karachi and elsewhere in Pakistan.

Despite General Zia's professed desire to Islamize the polity and society in Pakistan, he was very careful in dealing with the perks and privileges of the landed aristocracy, the bureaucracy and the business elite. The business elite was particularly comfortable with the Zia regime, as he provided them with welcome relief from Bhutto's 'Islamic Socialism'. The Bhutto era had been marked by arbitrary arrests of businessmen whom Prime Minister Bhutto disliked and by equally arbitrary nationalization of their properties.

Dinner parties hosted by the business and social elite in Karachi had a flair of their own. If one was invited for a dinner at 8 p.m., it would only be prudent to reach the venue around 10.30 p.m. I recall that just after our arrival in Karachi, Shanti and I reached one such dinner on time only to find the hosts were still bathing and had not even changed for dinner. Whisky and wine were the order of the day in Karachi parties in Zia's Pakistan, even as he piously proclaimed his commitment to ruling the country strictly according to Islamic laws. I have never enjoyed my drinks so much and so often anywhere in the world as in Karachi.

Pakistanis are tremendously hospitable people and the cuisine in parties is exquisite. But virtually every dish has meat in it. Since Shanti and my elder daughter Rukmini were strict vegetarians we did run across some problems when we reached Karachi. Most people in Karachi seemed to think that eating only vegetables without meat was somehow beneath their dignity. But interestingly enough, within a year or so of our reaching Karachi some of our friends realized that vegetarian food can actually be tasty, wholesome and healthy. The first converts to this belief were members of the Haroon family, who owned the *Dawn* newspaper. The two Haroon brothers, Hamid and Hussein, were a delightful study in contrasts. Hamid was a connoisseur of Hindustani and Sindhi classical music. He has one of the finest collections I have seen of ancient Indian art pieces and maps. He loved sub-continental cuisine. Politically, he disliked General Zia and was supportive of a return to democracy. He genuinely felt that Benazir would provide the right kind of democratic leadership for the country. Hussein was, on the other hand, a true representative of the old landed aristocracy. He still adhered to the values and norms of the aristocratic and rich politicians who were drafted into the Executive Councils in British India. He would personally supervise the layout of some of the finest English and French cuisine, laced with the best French wines. Hussein was quite comfortable with General Zia's rule and even became Speaker of the Sindh Assembly in the Zia dispensation. The two brothers and their charming and gracious mother, like many other wonderful people, really made life so easy and comfortable for us in Karachi. All of them remain people whose friendship Shanti and I really cherish.

The early 1980s were marked in Pakistan by General Zia's ban on political rallies and processions. Politicians were permitted to speak and address gatherings only in buildings and not in public places. To discredit the politicians a campaign to label them 'drawing room politicians' was started. The Americans were everywhere and made no bones of the fact that they did not want the politicians to create trouble for Zia, with agitations and calls for democracy. I recall a senior American diplomat in Karachi acknowledging to me that as far as they were concerned they knew that General Zia was a ruthless dictator. But they did not want his attention to be diverted from bleeding the Soviet Union in Afghanistan because of domestic political concerns. The American recalled what President Roosevelt had said about Nicaraguan dictator, Anastasio Samoza: 'He may be an SOB. But he is *our* SOB.' Benazir was then under house arrest and the leadership of the PPP was in the hands of her mother, Nusrat Bhutto. Nusrat was a charming lady but not the sort of leader who could rally the public, or set the Indus River on fire with her oratory. She did grace some of the receptions I hosted. Nusrat Bhutto was aware that Mrs Indira Gandhi had let General Zia know in no uncertain terms that, while she did not know either of the Bhutto ladies personally and did not wish to interfere in Pakistan's internal affairs, she would be very unhappy if any personal harm should come to the two women leaders in Pakistan. It is interesting that despite her being a hard realist, Mrs Gandhi seemed to have a rapport with and regard for women political leaders, whether it was Margaret Thatcher, Sirimavo Bandarnaike, or Nusrat Bhutto.

During a dinner meeting in Karachi, I once remarked to Nusrat Bhutto that her husband was known to be an astute political leader and a shrewd judge of human beings. What then led him to make such a big miscalculation about the propensities of General Zia? Nusrat acknowledged that her husband was only human and had been taken in by General Zia's protestations about his fidelity and his repeated assertions that he was a pious Muslim with no political inclinations. She recalled that when General Zia was Corps Commander in Multan, he used to constantly criticize other Generals for being privately critical of Bhutto, whenever he met the then President. He would repeatedly tell Bhutto that he (Bhutto) was the real saviour of Pakistan after the 1971 Bangladesh debacle. He also used to flatter Bhutto's ego by even personally supervising the security arrangements for the President, whenever Bhutto visited Multan. Bhutto, being only human, got carried away by Zia's flattery. It was at that dinner meeting that I told Nusrat Bhutto that I was scheduled to accompany the then Lieutenant Governor of Delhi, Jagmohan, the next day for a meeting with General Zia. Nusrat remarked: 'When you are with him do observe his eyes and let me know what you think.' Intrigued by her remark, I spent the one-hour meeting that Governor Jagmohan had with General Zia looking closely at General Zia's eyes. When human beings smile there is invariably a twinkle in their eyes. What, however, struck me most was that there was no glint in General Zia's eyes when he smiled!

I met Nusrat Bhutto a few days later. She said that she had seen my meeting with General Zia on Pakistan television. 'What did you notice about the great man's eyes?' she asked. I told her that even when he smiled General Zia's eyes did not sparkle. They were instead cold and expressionless. 'Did they not remind you of the eyes of a cobra?' she asked. I was thunderstruck. What she said summed up the feeling one got looking at General Zia's eyes when he smiled. But to General Zia's credit it must be said that he knew how to run circles around gullible Indian journalists and peace activists, who strangely believed that muttering a few sweet nothings in Punjabi would melt the dictator's heart. Even a hardheaded film star like Shatrughan Sinha could not remain unmoved by Zia's impeccable politeness, his readiness to spare hours of his time for Indian guests and the careful psychological profiling that he ensured his staff had done of individual Indian visitors. But, it was perhaps Shatrughan Sinha alone amongst the many Indian visitors that Zia received, who had a friendship with Zia that flowed from the affection that Zia's young, handicapped daughter had for him. And Zia literally doted on his little girl. I also recall Sunil Gavaskar, who was captain of the Indian team during the disastrous tour of Pakistan in 1982, asking me in Rawalpindi if it would be all right for him to ask General Zia to grace the occasion when he was playing his hundredth cricket test in Lahore. I told Sunil that he was welcome to do so. Not surprisingly, Zia readily agreed and turned up to see Sunil open the Indian innings. If General Zia had found time to author a book on public relations based on his own practices, the book would undoubtedly have been a bestseller!

Zia managed the media in Pakistan with great skill. He was invariably present at any function organized by editors and newspaper proprietors. One could, however, not fail to be impressed by the courage and intellectual honesty of a large number of Pakistani journalists. The Karachi Press Club was virtually a nerve centre for pro-democracy activists. It was a place where fiery political speeches were made and Urdu poetry lampooning military rule was recited in colourful poetry reading sessions or *mushairas*. Many of the newspapers and their owners chose not to risk their well-being and avoided direct criticism of the military dictatorship. But the editors and senior journalistic staff of the *Dawn,* led by its far-sighted and urbane Editor Ahmed Ali Khan, were all people of unquestionable intellectual integrity. They knew how to convey their voices of dissent against military rule subtly but effectively in Pakistan's largest circulating English newspaper. It is to the credit of Hamid Haroon, who owns the newspaper group, that even in difficult times he did not ever interfere with the editorial freedom of his staff. There are very few newspaper proprietors in India who can take credit for giving their editorial staff and journalists such freedom and respecting their personal dignity. But it was the mass circulation Urdu press in Pakistan that faced subtle, but strong censorship. It is true that some Urdu newspapers, like the pro-PPP daily *Aman* edited by Afzal Siddiqui, showed a measure of independence. But large newspapers like the *Jang* and *Nawai Waqt* basically toed the Government line. While they were free to criticize lapses by the Government and even individual Ministers, personal criticism of General Zia, or the army establishment was strictly forbidden.

Despite General Zia's talk of Islamization, society in Pakistan basically remained liberal and moderate in the 1980s. But signs were emerging that the ISI-sponsored jihad in Afghanistan was laying the foundations of religious extremism and bigotry in the country. Armed student cadres of parties like the Jamaat-i-Islami were allowed to carry weapons to intimidate political rivals even in university campuses. Armed robberies became more frequent, as AK 47 rifles meant for the Afghan mujahideen found their way into the Karachi markets. At the start of my tenure in Karachi in January 1981, the security guards at the residences of the feudal elite carried somewhat antiquated 'twelve-bore' guns. When I left in 1985, guards carrying AK 47 rifles protected these residences. On my return to Pakistan as High Commissioner over a decade later, I found the AK 56 rifle was the weapon most commonly carried even by security guards in five star hotels. Political differences were sought to be resolved, more often than not, by recourse to violence. Zia's efforts to 'depoliticize' Pakistani society by banning mainstream political parties and open political gatherings led to the mushrooming of sectarian organizations. This inevitably resulted in increased Shia-Sunni confrontation. Rivalry between Saudi Arabia and Iran only exacerbated and widened this sectarian divide.

The most notable feature of Pakistan's politics has been the stranglehold of the rural feudal elite. Despite his socialist rhetoric, Zulfiqar Ali Bhutto, a member of Sind's rural landowning elite, never resorted to radical land reforms to effectively limit the power of the feudal landlords of Pakistan. The net result has been the continuing domination of Pakistan's politics by the country's landed aristocracy that virtually wields the power of life and death over their landless labour. Feudal families more often than not hedged their political bets by ensuring that at least one member of the family was associated with each major political party, the Pakistan People's Party (PPP) or the Pakistan Muslim League (PML). Upward social mobility in rural Pakistan has been rendered impossible. The big landlords call the shots. A politician like Ghulam Mustafa Jatoi, who was number two in Bhutto's Government and has been the country's interim Prime Minister, owns thousands of acres of agricultural land in rural Sind. A man of great personal charm, Jatoi was known to have a cosy relationship with the army hierarchy, which sought to build him up as an alternative to Benazir Bhutto. But when the Movement for the Restoration of Democracy led an agitation against Martial Law in 1983, politicians in Sind were drawn into the vortex of the agitation by the depth of anti-Punjabi sentiment that swept through rural Sind. It is this anti-Punjabi sentiment that has led some members of the landed aristocracy like Mumtaz Ali Bhutto to articulate the cause of increasing provincial autonomy and even call for a confederal structure for Pakistan. Others said to be close to the military establishment, like Jatoi, were drawn into the agitation and arrested.

The years of martial law under General Zia stifled legitimate and open political activity. This was a great pity, as the country was unable to go through a process of political evolution in which the aspirations of different sections of society could be accommodated and differences reconciled through dialogue and discussion. It was during this period that Pakistanis rather cynically started asserting they could do very little to take charge of their own destiny. They lamented that their fate was in the hands of the three all-powerful A's–Allah, Army and America. But I did make a number of good friends from amongst a wide cross section of politicians when I was in Karachi. These friendships included a warm and relaxed association with people across a wide political spectrum, ranging from ardent leftists like the Baluch leader Ghous Bux Bizenjo to the leader of the Jamaat-i-Islami in Karachi, the highly sophisticated and soft-spoken Professor Ghafoor Ahmed. Professor Ghafoor Ahmed was a muhajir from UP, who played a key role as Minister in General Zia's Government shortly after the 1977 coup in persuading General Zia to agree to the early opening of an Indian Consulate General in Karachi. His constituents were insistent that he should do this. Thus, even leaders from right-wing religious parties in Pakistan do have links with India that are not apparent in their rhetoric. Given such relationships, I was in a position to talk quite frankly to leaders of right-wing religious groups in Pakistan when I returned as High Commissioner about the damage they were doing to themselves and to those in India whom they claimed to defend, by their actions and irresponsible talk about jihad in Kashmir and elsewhere in India.

Despite possessing undoubted engineering ingenuity like their counterparts in India, the business elite in Pakistan did not really seek to invest in the development of a modern industrial infrastructure in their country. Bhutto's policies of arbitrary and vindictive nationalization only made the industrial climate even more uncertain. Adding to the industrial woes of Pakistan was the unrestricted smuggling of consumer goods ostensibly destined for Afghanistan. (The extent of this smuggling was manifested by the fact that shaving blades, razors and shaving cream were imported duty-free into Afghanistan and then smuggled into Pakistan in large quantities, even when the bearded Taliban ruled that country!) Thus, apart from the textile sector, the country's economic policies led to the neglect of other sectors of industrial development. By the 1970s, extensive modernization of the textile sector had made Pakistani exports of textiles competitive internationally. It was this competitiveness and the ancillary skills that were developed in areas like garment export that have enabled Pakistan to use its textile sector as an engine for export growth. Sadly, this modernization was not sustained and by the 1990s several textile mills were forced to face closure.

Nothing has been more debilitating to the emergence of a healthy and growing middle class in Pakistan than its feudal structure superimposed on the illusions in the mind of its military elite about Pakistan's endless strategic importance to the United States and the Western World. Successive Pakistani Governments have paid more attention to how they could forge regional and global alliances to attain 'parity' with India, rather than on promoting literacy, health and human development. I recall that in the 1980s one of my colleagues pointed out to a Finance Secretary of Pakistan that in the long term it would be difficult for Pakistan to sustain a healthy growth rate when national savings amounted to barely ten per cent of its GDP.

The reply that my young colleague received was typical of the mindset of the Pakistan bureaucracy. He was told: 'We Muslims have ruled the sub-continent for centuries. Rulers do not save—they spend. Savings are reflective of the insecurities in the mindset of petty traders *(banias)*.'

Pakistan and its people can be genuinely proud of the excellence they have achieved in three sports—cricket, hockey and squash, where no effort has been spared to allow national talents to develop to their full potential. And the credit for this should largely go to a Pakistani with great vision and dedication, Air Marshal Nur Khan. As a national hero of the 1965 conflict with India, Nur Khan had the stature to resist pressures and extend patronage to sportsmen of class and quality, not only as Chairman of Pakistan International Airlines, but also as head of various sporting bodies in Pakistan. He saw to it that cricket became a national passion and that those with talent would be rewarded. And in Imran Khan he found a talented figure with great capabilities to motivate and lead his players. The two together saw to it that the talent available in the streets across the country was tapped and mobilized. While the Indian cricket team has traditionally been predominantly drawn from those who have played for schools and universities in the country, one rarely finds a college graduate in the Pakistan team. What Nur Khan and Imran Khan have succeeded in doing is in seeing that even poor kids without much formal education can become national heroes. The contest between Pakistan and India in cricket has till recently been one between tough competitors who have no career other than cricket on the one hand and college educated middle class boys who start planning on how they will make their money after they leave the sporting arena, on the other. While the Pakistanis tried to snatch victory from the jaws of defeat, our boys tended to often lose their nerve when victory was in sight.

Kanwar Natwar Singh, our Ambassador to Pakistan, was paying a farewell visit to Karachi in March 1982, when Shanti and I joined him and his wife to witness an India-Pakistan hockey match in a packed Karachi stadium, with thousands of spectators determined to robustly cheer on their team. The spectators were wild with joy when a brilliant Pakistani team soundly thrashed the visiting Indians 7-1. I was later told that the Pakistan television cameras had gleefully focused its cameras on the Ambassador and on me with our crestfallen looks every time the talented Pakistani centre forward, Hassan Sardar, sounded the goal post. It was against this background that I agreed later that year, with some trepidation, to tie up all the arrangements for the visit of an Indian cricket team led by the legendary Sunil Gavaskar, who was unquestionably one of the best opening batsmen the world has ever seen. The charismatic Imran Khan led Pakistan and it soon became evident that we were in for a sound thrashing. Apart from a few solid batting performances by Gavaskar and Mohinder Amarnath, our boys just could not cope with the pace and swing of Imran, who was perhaps the best all-rounder the world has ever seen after Sir Garfield Sobers. Sadly, the Indian bowling was a one-man attack depending entirely on Kapil Dev. The other bowlers appeared to lack penetration. Imran invariably led by example and always had time to give tips to young debutants like Salim Malik. But even then one learnt from Pakistani commentators that Imran regarded the matches against India not merely as sporting encounters, but virtually as a jihad for Kashmir.

Our cricket team returned to Pakistan in 1984 after having won the cricket World Cup in 1983. The World Cup victory had done their confidence a lot of good. While virtually all the recognized batsmen performed wonderfully, the bowlers apart from the lion-hearted Kapil Dev again appeared to lack penetration. This tour had sadly to be cut short because of the assassination of Prime Minister Indira Gandhi on 31 October 1984. I could sense that the entire team was totally shocked by what had transpired when they came to sign the condolence book at the Consulate. Things do, however, now appear to be changing, with our cricketers, like our present-day hockey stars, showing increasing aggression, motivation and fighting spirit. It is also now noteworthy that those who emerge at the national level in cricket in India today are not almost exclusively college graduates, as they used to be in the past. But, we still have much to learn from Pakistan's seemingly endless ability to produce world-class fast bowlers.

It was during the visit of the cricket team in 1982 that I first set eyes on Nawaz Sharif, who had been appointed by the military authorities as a Minister in the Punjab Provincial Government. It was said in Lahore that General Zia had asked the Governor of Punjab, Lieutenant General Ghulam Jilani Khan, to create a new Muslim League Party with young leaders to take on Benazir Bhutto's PPP. Sharif's father was an industrialist who had been at the receiving end of notably vicious treatment from Zulfiqar Ali Bhutto. After some persuasion, the elder Sharif known as 'Abbaji' agreed that his elder son Nawaz, who was not too academically inclined and given to a passion for playing cricket, could join the new faction of the Muslim League that was backed by the army. Sharif told me that he wanted to host a 'small lunch' for our cricket team just before the Lahore test. The 'small lunch' was the first taste for me of Lahore hospitality Sharif-style—classic hospitality that I was to experience again when Prime Minister Vajpayee arrived on his famous 'bus yatra' to Lahore in February 1999. Like our cricket team, I was astounded to see around 4000 guests drawn from the elite of Lahore and the neighbouring towns of Punjab at the 'small lunch' that Sharif hosted!

Relations with Pakistan had become tense in 1983 and 1984. Indira Gandhi was impatient with General Zia's propensity to stir up Sikh separatism and terrorism in Punjab. When a group of Kashmiris belonging to the pro-independence Jammu and Kashmir Liberation Front kidnapped and killed Ravindra Mhatre, our Assistant High Commissioner in Birmingham, Mrs

Gandhi immediately concluded that there was Pakistani involvement. She responded by ordering the execution of JKLF activist Maqbool Bhatt, who had been awarded a death sentence for murder in India. Activists of the JKLF attacked my car just as it was entering the Consulate premises the very next day. It was a narrow escape for my driver and me. But the attackers smashed the flag car with iron crowbars and rained stones on the Consulate. The Chancery building had extensive glasswork and the glass was shattered. Oddly, even the normal complement of armed Pakistani security personnel was not around when the attack took place. It was evident that the attack enjoyed tacit Government support. Recognizing this, I refused to move the car from the Chancery entrance till the international media had arrived and photographed the damage. Reacting swiftly, Zia ordered the Chief Secretary of Sind to express regret and offer compensation for the damage caused. He was after all a master of managing public relations!

Despite the tensions and surveillance that one experienced in Karachi, my tenure there was in many ways unforgettable. People in Karachi were more often than not open and friendly. The liberal visa policy that we adopted, leading to hundreds of thousands of Pakistanis visiting India, gave them a totally new perspective about India. They learnt that the constant propaganda in the Urdu press that alleged the regular massacre and discrimination of Muslims in India was false. Though Indian films were banned, pirated video cassettes of these films often reached Karachi from Dubai even before the films were released in India for screening. Indian film icons like Amitabh Bachchan became household names. My daughters Priya and Rukmini studied at the American school and rarely felt uncomfortable with their Pakistani peers. Our Pakistani friends were warm and welcoming, and we even had car pool arrangements with our neighbours Hakim and Fiza Adamjee whose son Hafiz was Rukmini's classmate. We had a similarly friendly relationship with Shafkat Shah and his wife Nasreen, who had just returned from the United States. Their kids, like ours, studied in the American School. Shafkat was related to Mohammed Khan Junejo, a Muslim League leader, who later became Prime Minister of Pakistan, only to be sacked by General Zia for trying to act independently. Shafkat was later to become a Minister in General Musharraf's Cabinet but he resigned over Sind's share of the waters of the Indus. His brother Zulfi was of great help when the Indian cricket team visited Hyderabad.

Shanti's best friend in Karachi was Afifa Abid, the wife of a businessman, who like Shanti was learning sculpture in the Karachi Arts Council. I still recall how Shanti fasted during the month of Ramzan in 1985 just to keep Afifa company and to understand self-discipline based on faith. There were many in Karachi with whom one had ties that traced their origin to the days before the country was partitioned in August 1947. Pakistan's first Foreign Secretary, Ikramullah, joined the ICS in 1927 together with my father. His widow, Begum Shaista, was a leading social worker, who was touched by my father's gesture of sending her a photograph of the young ICS officers of the 1927 batch, taken when he and Mr Ikramullah were together in Cambridge. Abbas Khaleeli, an ICS officer from the Madras cadre who retired as Secretary to the Government of Pakistan, was yet another person whose family became very close friends. The widow of Pakistan's first Prime Minister, Begum Liaqat Ali Khan, fondly recalled the days when she used to play bridge with my mother in Delhi in the 1940s. But perhaps the most abiding friendships that we struck were with friends like the Haroons and Mazaris—friendships that still remain close today. It is one of Pakistan's great tragedies that politicians of unquestioned personal integrity like Sherbaz Khan Mazari found that they had no place in a structure in which politicians sought power by striking deals with the army. Mazari dwells on this phenomenon at some length in his book, *Journey to Disillusionment*, which he presented to me when Shanti and I

met him and his charming wife Soraya at a sumptuous lunch
they hosted for us in Karachi just after the Lahore Summit.
Sadly, the ISI and the military establishment found such
relationships entirely unsuitable and inconvenient for their
anti-Indian propaganda.

working with rajiv gandhi

My visits to Pakistan and association with Pakistani friends
continued for the five years that I spent in India after my return
from Karachi. When Rajiv Gandhi assumed power after his
sweeping election victory in 1984, he felt that he should make a
fresh effort to build bridges with all of India's neighbours,
including Pakistan. His accord in Punjab with Sant Longowal
restored the political and democratic processes in the State.
Pakistan-sponsored terrorism, however, continued. But it was
evident that the terrorists in Punjab were becoming more and
more isolated. General Zia was hugely relieved when Indira
Gandhi was assassinated. He found her son a far easier person
to deal with. Rajiv was determined that the tensions that had
risen from Pakistani fears that we would attack their nuclear
installations needed to be addressed. I had assisted Foreign
Secretary M.K. Rasgotra in negotiations that we had held with
Pakistan in 1984 to conclude an agreement not to attack each
other's nuclear facilities. Rajiv Gandhi was determined to see
that we made progress on this issue.

I visited Pakistan again in 1986 for Foreign Secretary-level
talks. The dialogue did keep the relationship on an even keel.
But tensions arose from time to time, as they did when India's
then army chief, General Sundarji, decided to hold huge
exercises code-named Operation Brass Tacks along the Indo-
Pakistan border in January 1987. These exercises, that involved
the use of armoured and mechanized formations in an offensive
mode, naturally caused concern in Pakistan. Pakistani fears were
heightened by the fact that even the normal communications,

that took place routinely between the Directors General of Military Operations, appeared to dry up. Arun Singh, a close associate of Prime Minister Rajiv Gandhi, then headed the Defence Ministry in New Delhi. Tensions escalated when Arun Singh authorized his military brass to brief the Indian press, claiming that Pakistani armoured formations had taken up menacing positions near the Indian border in Punjab. An irate Rajiv Gandhi ordered the Minister of State for External Affairs, Natwar Singh, to ascertain the precise locations of Pakistani strike formations from the White House and Kremlin, by using their satellite capabilities. Natwar Singh called in the American and Soviet Ambassadors separately and asked them to let us have their assessment of the Pakistani deployments on our borders. Within a day, both the White House and the Kremlin informed us that they were not able to find any evidence to substantiate our army's claims about menacing Pakistani troop movements. In the meantime, the Pakistanis had sought to convey through journalist Kuldip Nayar that we should recognize that they possessed nuclear weapons in their armoury. Nayar was informed about this in an unusual interview granted by Dr A.Q. Khan. The interview was 'arranged' by the then editor of the *Muslim* newspaper, Mushahid Hussain, who was known to be close to the military establishment. Nayar, however, did not formally convey this to our Government. The text of the interview was published in the *Observer* newspaper in the UK some weeks later.

When General Zia died in mysterious circumstance in an air crash in 1988, there was concern in India about the restoration of democracy in Pakistan. Zia's successor as President, the crusty former bureaucrat Ghulam Ishaq Khan, and the then Army Chief, General Mirza Aslam Beg, were known to be viscerally anti-Indian and very averse to granting a role to Benazir Bhutto in governing the country. But despite the odds, the Pakistan People's Party (PPP) led by Benazir Bhutto swept the polls. Recalling the old adage that Pakistan's fate is

determined by the three 'A's, Allah, Army and America, a
Pakistani friend of mine then remarked: 'One does not know
how Allah feels about Benazir assuming power. The Army
certainly does not favour her. And the Americans know that
after what happened to her father she will be more than friendly
to them.' The Army supported Benazir's appointment as the
Prime Minister only after she agreed that its choice, Sahabzada
Yakub Khan, would be the Foreign Minister. She was also forced
to agree that the military establishment would have a decisive
say and veto on relations with India and Afghanistan and on
nuclear policy. Benazir had assiduously cultivated the
Americans. With the Soviet Union showing every sign of getting
out of Afghanistan, the White House was quite willing to live
with a modicum of democracy in Pakistan. Many of Bhutto's
supporters in Pakistan felt that the CIA had colluded with
General Zia in Bhutto's overthrow in 1977 because of his
determination to develop nuclear weapons in Pakistan. But I
have often wondered if his attempted flirtations with the Soviet
Union had also not irked Henry Kissinger, who threatened to
make a 'horrible example' of him.

When I visited Pakistan with Rajiv Gandhi on two occasions
in 1989, I was perhaps one of the few in the visiting
delegation—apart from my childhood friend, Satish Chandra,
who then headed the Pakistan Desk in our Foreign office—who
were not carried away by the hype and euphoria that marked
these visits. (Satish is presently India's Deputy National Security
Adviser). Both Satish and I knew that while Benazir was keen to
discard some of Zia's policies, her own room for manoeuvre and
flexibility was limited. Rajiv Gandhi later told me that she was
reluctant to speak to him openly in closed rooms because she
feared that they had been bugged by the ISI and President Ishaq
Khan. He also knew that trouble was brewing in Kashmir, as the
Intelligence Bureau Chief, M.K. Narayanan, had showed him
large caches of arms that had been smuggled across the Line of
Control from 1988 onwards. Rajiv was, in fact, planning to

bring back a substantial number of troops deployed with the Indian Peace Keeping Force in Sri Lanka by mid-1989 to deal with the emerging situation in Jammu and Kashmir.

I met Rajiv Gandhi for the last time in September 1990 when he was Leader of the Opposition and the V.P. Singh Government had packed me off as High Commissioner to Cyprus. He recalled what I had told him about Benazir when he had visited Islamabad the previous year and said that he was shocked by her virulent rhetoric on Kashmir. More importantly, he told me that he had warned the then Prime Minister, V.P. Singh, that he should not seek to divert attention from the problems he faced in dealing with his differences with his Deputy Prime Minister, Devi Lal, by escalating tensions with Pakistan. Northern India was literally in flames then, because of caste riots that followed the Government's decision to enhance reservations in Government jobs for the 'backward classes'. Expressing regret at the manner in which V.P. Singh's policies based on political expediency were polarizing the country on caste lines, Rajiv acerbically noted: 'He (V.P. Singh) is emerging as the most divisive element in Indian politics since Jinnah.' Rajiv was also severely critical of how national interests had been sacrificed and secessionism given a boost by the decision to release hard-core terrorists in Kashmir to secure the release of the kidnapped daughter of the then Home Minister, Mufti Mohammed Sayeed.

vajpayee's bus yatra

When I returned to Pakistan as High Commissioner, I found that the entire relationship had become bitter and acrimonious. Civilized dialogue had become virtually impossible. In the talks between the Foreign Secretaries that had been held before my arrival, the Pakistan side led by the hawkish Shamshad Ahmad made it amply clear that there could be no progress on promoting cooperation or resolving differences on issues like the demarcation of the border in Sir Creek or the Tulbul

Navigation Project till the Kashmir issue was addressed to Pakistan's satisfaction. But my first priority was to see that the forthcoming visit of Prime Minister Vajpayee to Lahore by bus went off successfully. The Foreign Office was obviously none too enthusiastic about the visit. The Foreign Minister, Sartaj Aziz, was a well-meaning economist who was out of his depth as Foreign Minister. Relations with India were entirely managed by Foreign Secretary Shamshad Ahmad and Additional Secretary Tariq Aziz, who appeared to believe that India would wilt under the force of Pakistan's propaganda that Kashmir was a 'nuclear flashpoint' that had to be resolved to Pakistan's satisfaction. Shamshad, who was known to be a protégé of the military establishment and the ISI, obviously shared the views of his mentors that India would disintegrate as it continued to 'bleed' in Jammu and Kashmir and elsewhere. I learnt that Nawaz himself realized that Pakistan's policies in Afghanistan and India were causing the country considerable damage. But, given his Muslim League background he could not resist the temptation of playing footsie with terrorist groups like the Lashkar-e-Taiba or assisting the remnants of the Sikh separatist movement in Punjab.

Prime Minister Vajpayee's decision to visit Lahore in February 1999 was a well-considered one. The international community was seriously concerned over what it perceived were the growing tensions between India and Pakistan after the May 1998 nuclear tests. Further, it has always been Vajpayee's ambition that he should achieve in foreign policy something that even Jawaharlal Nehru had been unable to do. Unlike other leaders of his party, Vajpayee genuinely holds Nehru in high respect for the warmth and attention that Nehru had devoted to him in his first tenure as a young Member of Parliament in the 1950s. When I met him just before I left for Islamabad, I could sense that despite the deep misgivings within the country and particularly in his own Party, Vajpayee wanted to make progress and lay the foundations for opening a new chapter in our relations with Pakistan. Given my past experience I did have my own scepticism about what could be achieved. But I was determined to spare no effort to see that the Prime Minister's visit was hailed as a major effort for peace and reconciliation. There were clear rivalries within the Pakistan establishment about how the visit should be handled. Shamshad and his lieutenant, Tariq Altaf, saw the visit as an unnecessary diversion from their 'core agenda'. They wanted to see that nothing substantive emerged from the visit and made every effort to queer the pitch.

Luckily for me I had an excellent team of colleagues in Islamabad. We soon got together and the Deputy High Commissioner, Sharat Sabharwal, took charge of all administrative and protocol arrangements, enabling me to concentrate on the substance, political content and media profile for the visit. It soon became clear to me that Nawaz Sharif himself had misgivings about his Foreign Office's approach to the visit. When I reached Lahore to finalize arrangements for the visit, Prime Minister Nawaz Sharif's Office told me that the Governor of Punjab, Shahid Hamid, and not the Foreign Office, would coordinate all the arrangements for the visit to Lahore with me. Governor Hamid had obviously received instructions from Nawaz Sharif to spare no effort to see that arrangements for the visit were tied up in meticulous detail. He and I went together to the Wagah Border to actually tie up all details and personally participate in a full dress rehearsal of the arrival ceremonials. In the meantime, a team of officials from Delhi had arrived to tie up the protocol, media and security arrangements. The cooperation that we received from our hosts was exemplary. I started breathing easier and felt reassured that the visit would go off smoothly.

Around this time, I got instructions from Delhi that I should lead the team of officials to finalize the joint statement to be issued at the end of the visit. I felt a mere joint statement for the press would not do justice to the importance of the visit. I urged the Pakistani side that we should have a declaration spelling out the shared vision of the two leaders for the future relationship. The ever-negative Tariq Altaf peremptorily rejected this suggestion saying that when there were such vast differences over Kashmir it would be meaningless to talk of a 'shared vision' of the two countries. Brajesh Misra had meanwhile arrived in Lahore. He used his own channels with Nawaz Sharif to see that Altaf was overruled. But, negotiating the text of the joint declaration turned out to be a torturous affair. Mercifully, Joint Secretary Vivek Katju, who headed the Pakistan Division in the Indian Foreign Office, was more than a match for Altaf in standing firm. Katju eventually saw to it that he could prevail on the negotiating table by a sheer process of stonewalling and attrition. The Joint Declaration was finally given its finishing touches just before the conclusion of the visit. Just as we were concluding the text, we received word that the Army Chief, General Ved Malik, had been insistent that the text should carry a reference to terrorism. Even this was achieved, after we agreed to meet a matching insertion by the Pakistani side.

While looking after Vajpayee and his delegation was relatively straightforward, one really had one's hands full making arrangements for nearly 300 media persons who had flown in from Delhi. Accompanying Vajpayee on the bus were over a dozen prominent Indians drawn from different walks of life. They included persons like artist Satish Gujral and his wife Kiran, film stars Dev Anand and Shatrughan Sinha, singer Mahendra Kapur and the ubiquitous Kuldip Nayar. The commencement of the visit was not too propitious. The three Service Chiefs led by Army Chief General Musharraf avoided attending the arrival ceremonies. And they made it a point to be without their headgear when they met Vajpayee at a reception in Governor's mansion. General Musharraf was clearly in no mood to be seen saluting the visiting Head of Government of a country he so fervently hated. The lavish dinner that Nawaz Sharif had organized in the Lahore Fort was delayed, as the

Lahore Police fought running battles with protestors from the fundamentalist Jamaat-i-Islami, who were bent on blockading the route that Vajpayee's motorcade was to take. When we finally reached the venue of the dinner over one and a half hours late, the Lahore fort was filled with tear gas that had been used by the police against the demonstrators. Ambassadors from third countries who had been invited were at the receiving end of tear gas shells as they proceeded to the Lahore Fort for dinner.

The official talks the next day were confined to generalities, with both sides expressing their respective views and concerns, but agreeing to expand contacts and interaction. The future course of action was set out in the joint declaration that had been negotiated with the Pakistan Foreign Office. But the entire climate during the summit was enjoyable and relaxed. In symbolic terms, the most important event was the visit that Vajpayee made to the Minar-e-Pakistan, the monument set up at the site of the meeting on 23 March 1940, where the Muslim League led by Jinnah set out its demand for a separate Muslim homeland in the Indian sub-continent. This visit was meant to finally bury misgivings in Pakistan that India was not somehow reconciled to its very existence as a separate nation state. Vajpayee had visited the memorial to the greatest Sikh ruler of the 19th century, Maharaja Ranjit Singh, the previous evening. Nawaz Sharif's lunch just after the official talks was enlivened with the Punjab Police band playing some enchanting light music of 1950s and 1960s vintage from India. Nawaz and his wife Kulsum loved this music, though neither Vajpayee nor Jaswant Singh were able to respond to Nawaz Sharif's queries about whether they were able to identify the tunes played. This task was left to me, as one of my lifelong passions has been my fondness for old Hindi musical hits. I found that Lt. General Moinuddin Haider, then Governor of Sind, who was seated between Mr Jaswant Singh and me at the banquet hosted by Nawaz Sharif, shared my fondness for old Hindi film songs, especially those sung by Lata Mangeshkar and Mohammed Rafi.

Haider later became Interior Minister of Pakistan, when General Musharraf seized power. He struck me as being one of those rare officers in the Pakistan army who had a relatively realistic and sober appraisal of relations with India.

Vajpayee's foster daughter, Namrita, developed a warm relationship with Mrs Nawaz Sharif—a relationship reinforced with the love that the Pakistan Prime Minister's wife had for Indian film and classical music. It was a pleasure to deal with Namrita (whom Shanti and I had known from the days that Vajpayee was Foreign Minister) and her husband Ranjan Bhattacharya. Both of them were very relaxed, friendly and informal, unlike the boorish, arrogant and officious family members and personal staff who sometimes accompany visiting Indian dignitaries. Vajpayee himself was in a laidback and contemplative mood. Just after the lunch that followed the official talks, he asked whether there was any written text for his speech at the civic reception that had been scheduled for the evening. I strongly urged that he should speak extempore and not allow himself to be programmed by anyone else. His speech in which he spoke emotionally and recited a couplet he had composed expressing abhorrence of war and conflict deeply impressed even the cynics who were present. Even a hard-boiled person like the Pakistan Information Minister, Mushahid Hussain, was so impressed that he agreed to the speech being played on two occasions on the state-run Pakistan television. There have been very few national leaders in India who could match Mr Vajpayee's oratory, his intrinsic generosity, his readiness to listen to dissenting views, or his wry sense of humour. It is really these characteristics that have led to his being treated with affection and respect all across India.

The Lahore Declaration signed by Vajpayee and Nawaz Sharif voiced a mutual commitment to resolve all outstanding issues, including Jammu and Kashmir, while reiterating their commitment to the Simla Agreement of July 1972. The two Prime Ministers agreed to intensify the 'composite and integrated' dialogue process between the two countries. An apparently innocuous part of the Declaration reaffirms the commitment of the two Prime Ministers to achieve the objectives laid down in the SAARC vision statement 2020. I was particularly keen on having this commitment voiced, as Vision Statement 2020 commits the countries of South Asia to a process of progressive economic integration leading to the establishment of a South Asian Economic Community similar to the European Economic Community by 2020. This alone, in my view, could lead to the creation of an environment of trust, cooperation and confidence that would enable us to address and seek to resolve complex issues like Jammu and Kashmir. The Prime Ministers also pledged to take immediate steps for nuclear risk reduction, to discuss nuclear concepts and doctrines and develop Confidence Building Measures (CBMs) aimed at the prevention of conflict.

Brajesh Misra recognized that it was imperative that India and Pakistan should develop a wide range of CBMs if the concerns of the international community about tensions between India and Pakistan were to be assuaged and tensions were not allowed to get out of hand. India and Pakistan agreed at Lahore to provide each other advance notification of missile tests and to conclude bilateral agreement on the subject. They agreed to abide by their respective unilateral moratoria on nuclear testing. They also agreed to conclude an agreement to prevent incidents at sea involving their naval ships and aircraft. It was decided that not only would communication links between the Directors General of Military Operations be upgraded and improved, but direct links would also be established between designated field commanders. In informal gatherings at the residence of our Air Attaché, Group Captain Jaiswal, after the Lahore Summit, I suggested to officers of the Pakistan Air Force that there should be direct links between the Air Operations Staffs of the two countries. The response I received was positive.

Amidst all these developments, the one person who was quietly sceptical about anything enduring being achieved was our soft-spoken Foreign Secretary, Krishnan Raghunath. I was, however, somewhat taken aback at the manner in which a person with an army background like External Affairs Minister Jaswant Singh got so carried away by developments of the moment. He seemed to be more interested in obtaining a replica of a bronze statuette in the Governor's residence than on issues of substance. Nawaz Sharif had, in a rather tongue in cheek manner, expressed his admiration for the rather colourful Rajasthani turban that Jaswant Singh had sported at the banquet in Lahore Fort. Taking what Nawaz said at face value, Jaswant Singh promptly offered to send him a set of hand-stitched turbans from Rajasthan as soon as he returned to India. He duly did so, along with a personal hand-written letter saying that the gift of turbans reflected the high esteem in which he personally held Nawaz Sharif. Not surprisingly, a bemused Nawaz Sharif did not reply. What surprised me about this extraordinary gesture by Jaswant Singh was that he simply did not seem to realize the symbolism of such presentations of turbans to the executive head of a none too friendly neighbouring country.

It was quite obvious to me during the Lahore Summit that Pakistani democracy had a long way to go before it matured and that the tolerance and mutual respect that must exist between the ruling dispensation and the Opposition in a mature country were missing. Senior representatives of Opposition parties were not invited to any of the functions hosted by the Government. As Leader of the Opposition, Benazir Bhutto was naturally keen to formally meet the Indian Prime Minister. But Nawaz Sharif did not want to have her anywhere near the summit venue. I did receive word from Benazir that she would be happy to meet the Prime Minister if invited. I consulted Vajpayee and conveyed that he would be happy to receive her. But it soon became evident that our hosts were not at all keen for Benazir to share the limelight in Lahore. In the event, the meeting with Benazir did not materialize. I did not want the gains achieved in the Lahore Summit to be eroded because of domestic political opposition in Pakistan. I met Benazir a few days after the summit at her residence in Karachi. She seemed satisfied by the fact that the Lahore Declaration had reaffirmed commitment to the provisions of the Simla Agreement signed by her father. But she was highly sceptical about the '*Mullah, Madrassa, Military* combine' allowing any movement forward in relations with India. Her prediction proved right.

kargil and the coup

Within days of the Lahore Summit, Nawaz Sharif again started playing footsie with Sikh separatists and fishing in troubled waters in Punjab. He had appointed the former Director General of the ISI, Lieutenant General Javed Nasir, as head of a so-called 'Pakistan Gurudwara Prabhandak Committee'. Javed Nasir was reputed to have played a key role in engineering the Bombay Blasts of 1993, and Nawaz had been forced to sack him, reportedly because of American pressure, after those terrorist blasts. Nasir used his new appointment to bring extremists from groups like the Babbar Khalsa International and the International Sikh Youth Federation from the United States, Canada and the United Kingdom to Pakistan at the same time as a visit by a large group of Sikh pilgrims from India. Banners hailing 'Khalistan' were put up in gurudwaras in Lahore and elsewhere being visited by the Indian Sikh pilgrims. Provocative statements were made in the presence of high Pakistani dignitaries calling on Sikhs in India to revolt against the 'Hindu' Government. Nawaz Sharif, like his mentor General Zia before him, decided to personally receive the visiting Sikh pilgrims in the presence of all those secessionists brought in from across the world by General Javed Nasir. It was suggested to me that as Indian High Commissioner it would be appropriate for me to be present on the occasion. But notwithstanding all the prevailing hype about the 'Lahore spirit', I avoided going to Lahore for the meeting. I certainly did not want to be present when the Pakistan Prime Minister was receiving Sikh pilgrims from India in the presence of rabid secessionists from the United States, United Kingdom and elsewhere. Many of the pilgrims from India also found the Pakistani behaviour distasteful. To add insult to injury, ISI agents mercilessly beat up an attaché from the High Commission, who was liaison officer with the pilgrims from India, just outside the Dera Sahib Gurudwara in Lahore. He was unconscious when his colleagues took him to a nearby hospital.

Even though the Simla Agreement called on both countries to eschew hostile propaganda against each other, Pakistan television stepped up its propaganda tirade against India for alleged atrocities in Jammu and Kashmir just after the Lahore Summit. General Nasir and other luminaries started coming out with learned articles about how it was only a question of time before an Indian army worn out by the jihad in Kashmir would call it quits and leave Kashmir. It is precisely such propaganda and delusions flowing from it that leads many Pakistanis to believe that they could avenge Bangladesh by 'bleeding India with a thousand cuts'. One manifestation of this mindset that afflicts even supposedly liberal Pakistanis emerged in a meeting I had at a Lahore Hotel with Jugnu, the wife of the editor of the weekly *Friday Times*, Najm Sethi. I had barely been introduced to her by Lahore journalist Imtiaz Alam, when Jugnu burst out with the comment: 'You Indians will leave Kashmir once we see that enough body bags of your soldiers there are flown back to their homes.'

While ordinary people, particularly in the Punjab Province, regarded Hindus as being 'different' in the 1980s, the propaganda by the Urdu Press and Pakistan television had so vitiated the atmosphere in the 1990s that Indians, and particularly Hindus, were regarded by ordinary Pakistanis, especially in Punjab, as ogres who did nothing apart form indulging in rape and pillage against Muslims in Kashmir and elsewhere in India. The syllabus for instruction and history lessons in Pakistani schools and colleges is deliberately oriented to promote hatred towards Hindus. Hatred against the *Ahle Yahud* (Jews) and the *Ahle Hanud* (Hindus) was openly advocated in newspapers, books and in statements by leaders of jihadi groups like the Lashkar-e-Taiba. The only redeeming feature is that many Pakistanis get a totally different view of India from watching the growing number of Indian television channels. Indian films and television channels do far more to correct misperceptions about India in the minds of ordinary Pakistanis than any effort by the Indian Government can hope to achieve. But, in the ultimate analysis, such perceptions can change only when the Governments of both countries decide to end hostile propaganda against each other and actively promote greater human interaction.

All this was happening at a time when unknown to us, a few thousand soldiers of Pakistan's Northern Light Infantry were crossing the Line of Control and climbing the high peaks of Kargil in an operation designed to cut off our lines of communication to Northern Kashmir. The obvious aim of this military operation was to make it impossible for us to link up with and supply our army formations in Ladakh and the Siachen Glacier. General Musharraf had, in the meanwhile, made his views about the Lahore Summit clear in a meeting of the English Speaking Union in Karachi in mid-April 1999, barely a few weeks after it took place. Describing what transpired in the Summit as 'hot air', Musharraf asserted that in his view India was a 'hegemonic power'. He significantly added that 'low intensity conflict' with India would continue even if the Kashmir issue were resolved. This statement only confirmed the assessment that my predecessor Satish Chandra had made of Musharraf when he was appointed army chief. Satish had then described Musharraf as being ambitious, devious and virulently anti-Indian. Satish had said that Musharraf's appointment was bad news for India-Pakistan relations and predicted that Musharraf was a General who would not be averse to overthrowing the democratic dispensation in his country. We later learnt that it was Musharraf who masterminded the Kargil operation and persuaded Nawaz Sharif to go along in October 1998. By the second week of May 1999, it became obvious to us that there had been a serious lack of vigilance on our part, leading to unidentified Pakistanis crossing the Line of Control and threatening our supply routes to Northern Kashmir.

After attending a meeting of Indian Ambassadors to Central Asian Countries convened by Jaswant Singh in Turkmenistan, I reached Delhi around 19 May, only to be told to be present the next morning at a high-level briefing by the Army Chief, General Malik, that was attended by the Prime Minister, Defence Minister Fernandes, National Security Adviser Brajesh Misra and others. It was at this briefing that the extent of the Pakistani intrusion across the Line of Control in Kargil became clear. As a professional soldier, General Malik was unwilling to set a time schedule for expelling the intruders, but vowed his boys would do so, whatever it took to get the job done. It was also felt that air support would be necessary to let the Pakistanis know that we meant business. The Cabinet Committee on Security approved the Army Chief's request for air support the next morning, and I was asked to return to Islamabad immediately as air strikes were scheduled to commence shortly thereafter. But in approving the air strikes, Prime Minister Vajpayee was insistent that under no circumstances should the Indian Air Force cross the Line of Control, thus making close air support both difficult and hazardous, given the proximity of the positions to be attacked to the Line of Control. But the political and diplomatic gains that we achieved by this decision of respecting the sanctity of the Line of Control outweighed the disadvantages inherent in limitations placed on the use of air power.

The first few days after the air strikes commenced were distinctly uncomfortable. The downing of two MIG fighters, the capture of an Indian Air Force pilot, Flight Lieutenant Nachiketa, and the shooting down of a helicopter gunship that was captured live by television cameras, overjoyed the Pakistani establishment. But Pakistani diplomatic strategy soon became evident to us. The diplomatic aim was to say that the Line of Control was not properly defined or appropriately demarcated and that the positions occupied in the Kargil heights by the mujahideen were really in an area where there were doubts about the exact location of the Line of Control. Hence what was needed were talks to determine precisely where the Line of Control lay in the Kargil Sector. This was the ploy that Foreign Minister Sartaj Aziz sought to adopt when he visited New Delhi in June 1999. I warned New Delhi about this Pakistani ploy and urged that it should be effectively rebutted by furnishing foreign Governments and the media with the maps that had been signed by the military commanders of India and Pakistan in 1972. The Line of Control was very precisely defined and delineated in these maps. It was only a matter of time before the Pakistani bluff was called. The United States, the European Union and the G 8 called on Pakistan to respect the sanctity of the Line of Control and end its intrusion in Kargil. But by the time Nawaz Sharif left for Washington on 4 July, the Indian Army had succeeded in retaking the strategic heights overlooking the Srinagar-Leh road, with the capture of strategic hilltops like Toololing and Tiger Hill. Considerable blood would have had to be shed if the Pakistanis were to be pushed back from all the positions they had occupied. But the continued occupation of these positions would have been costly and meaningless for the Pakistan army in strategic terms, once the positions overlooking the Srinagar-Leh road were retaken by the Indian army in what must truly be regarded as a remarkable feat in the annals of mountain warfare.

Life in Pakistan was pretty tense during the Kargil conflict. But once the conflict started, my colleagues and I decided that we would go about our normal work. Pakistani visa applicants were treated with extra consideration and courtesy and all of us continued our normal diplomatic activities. The Lahore-Delhi bus service and train and air services between India and Pakistan continued uninterrupted. The Pakistanis were made to feel that while they were all excited about the conflict in Kargil, we were so confident that we would prevail that it was business as usual for us. But behind this façade it was evident to us in Islamabad that there was every chance of matters escalating. Counselor Syed Akbarrudin, who is one of the brightest young officers that I have known in the Indian Foreign Service, quietly ensured that should the need arise we would be in a position to move the entire staff and their families into the Chancery premises, where we had stocked enough fuel for our generators and food to last us for over two months. Not even the staff members of the High Commission were aware of this contingency plan. Deputy High Commissioner Sharat Sabharwal, who had done so much to help me during the Lahore Summit, had left on a posting to Geneva. His successor Sudhir Vyas, an IIT graduate, arrived just before the Kargil conflict was drawing to an end. Luckily for me, Sudhir was also an extremely competent, savvy and dedicated official.

A few days after a MIG 23 was downed by a surface-to-air missile and its pilot, Flight Lieutenant Nachiketa, was captured, Nawaz Sharif grandiosely announced that Nachiketa was being released and handed over to the Indian High Commissioner. An excited Tariq Altaf called me and told me about the announcement and said that the pilot would soon be handed over to me. Smelling a rat, I asked Tariq where I was supposed to take charge of Nachiketa and whether the media would be present. When Tariq told me that the media would be present, I saw red and said: 'Tariq, if you think I am going to allow you to make a media monkey of an officer of the Indian Air Force, you are sadly mistaken. There is no way I am coming to the Foreign Office if there is even one media person present anywhere in sight.' The entire world media in Islamabad had gathered in the

Foreign Office to watch the spectacle of a captured Indian Air Force pilot being handed over to me—an effort to reverse what had happened when General Niazi surrendered before the world media to General Arora in Dhaka in December 1971. What the Pakistanis had not bargained for was my refusal to fall for their bait. My calculation was that having announced that they would be releasing Nachiketa, the Pakistanis were no longer in a position to hold him indefinitely. After checking with Delhi, I suggested that Nachiketa could be handed over to the ICRC representatives without any photo opportunities for the media. The ICRC would then drive him over to the High Commission. This finally happened late at night. Early next morning, we put Nachiketa in an Embassy car and drove him across the border accompanied by the Air and Naval Attachés in the High Commission. The young pilot was touched when Prime Minister Vajpayee and his chief, the highly respected Air Chief Marshal Tipnis, spoke to him just before he left Islamabad.

The Kargil conflict came to an end with Nawaz Sharif's visit to the White House on 4 July, where he was virtually read the riot act by President Clinton. I was attending the Independence Day Reception at the residence of US Ambassador Bob Milam, where Musharraf and a whole lot of Pakistani dignitaries were present. Maleeha Lodhi, then editor of the *News*, spoke to me and asked me what I thought of the Nawaz visit. I had remained totally silent throughout the Kargil conflict and felt that the time had perhaps come to speak out. I told her: 'Maleeha, this is the beginning of the end game for Pakistan in Kargil.' The ever-vigilant Maleeha went back to her office, published my comments as headlines on the morning of July 5 and penned her own editorial entitled, 'End Game?' The Kargil adventure was a military, strategic and diplomatic disaster for Pakistan. But one doubts if its military establishment learnt any enduring lessons from what transpired. The disaster led to Musharraf having to run around cantonments in Pakistan trying to explain to his officers what had happened and how an army that claimed to have scored a major strategic triumph had to ignominiously pull back. He naturally blamed Nawaz Sharif. Touched to the quick, an irate Nawaz sought to ease out Musharraf, only to find that the person whom he had personally picked and appointed as Army Chief had outsmarted and eventually ousted him.

We have handled our post-Kargil publicity most unimaginatively. It should surely have been possible to invite foreign academics and military analysts to see the battle sites and get a first-hand idea of what the Indian Army had achieved during the Kargil conflict. Pushing out heavily armed intruders of the Pakistan Army from high Himalayan hilltops by direct and frontal assaults is a feat any professional army and nation can be proud of. There was also the highly skilful and imaginative use of artillery to blast mountain top positions with 155 mm Bofors Howitzers. There are not even a handful of armies in the world today whose soldiers would have been prepared to so readily sacrifice their lives in such an endeavour.

Indian diplomacy went through many strange twists and turns during Kargil. But perhaps the most mysterious and inexplicable was the role of R.K. Misra, who was used as a 'back channel' for communication with Nawaz Sharif. Misra started his career as a journalist and a Member of Parliament with Communist inclinations. But he soon found his way to edit a newspaper owned by a leading business house. He visited Pakistan and met Nawaz Sharif on a number of occasions during the Kargil conflict. Such contacts are not unusual in relationships that are as complicated as those between India and Pakistan. But what was unusual about Misra's appointment was that he did not have a clue about the provisions of basics like the Simla Agreement and past negotiations between India and Pakistan. According to his Pakistani counterpart, Niaz Naik, Misra had indicated in one of their meetings in Delhi during the Kargil conflict that New Delhi would agree to 'adjustments' in the Line of Control that would eventually lead to the Line of

Control being moved to the Chenab river basin. (Such an 'adjustment' would have resulted in the entire Kashmir valley being handed over to Pakistan!) Naik claimed that it was on this basis that Nawaz Sharif was proposing to visit Delhi on his return journey to Pakistan from a visit to China. Misra vehemently rejects Naik's assertion, but refused to appear and testify about his role before the Kargil Committee that was set up to inquire into the handling of the conflict. Naik is too accomplished a diplomat to go so wrong in his account of what had transpired.

Throughout the Kargil conflict, Nawaz Sharif personally recognized the importance of sounding me out and ascertaining my thinking. Apart from meeting his Interior Minister, Chaudhury Shujaat, I remained in touch with a young Muslim League Member of the National Assembly who was close to Sharif. It was clear to us that while Nawaz Sharif had okayed the Kargil adventure, he had been seriously misled by his adventuristic army chief about its strategic and diplomatic implications. It was also my assessment that having learnt the folly of trying to take on India militarily, Nawaz would henceforth be far more pragmatic in dealing with us. I conveyed to him that while we felt betrayed by what had transpired we had no desire to embarrass him personally. But things were heating up between Nawaz and Musharraf. Matters came to a head when Musharraf decided to suspend the Corps Commander Quetta, Lieutenant General Tariq Parvez, for the latter's allegedly unauthorized contacts with the Prime Minister. New Delhi was made aware of the growing tensions between the Prime Minister and the Army Chief when these developments were taking place. But no one expected Nawaz Sharif to act in the precipitate manner he did in endeavouring to sack his army chief when the latter was flying back from an official trip to Sri Lanka. It was a foolhardy and ill-advised move, because prior to his departure for Sri Lanka Musharraf had not only advised his Chief of General Staff, Lieutenant General Mohammed Aziz

Khan, and the Corps Commander Rawalpindi, Lieutenant General Mehmood Ahmad, on what needed to be done if Nawaz should seek to remove him, but he also had kept the 111 Brigade, that historically stages coups d'etat, ready to strike at short notice. Even the Americans and British were caught by surprise by the events of 12 October. The American Ambassador had left a week earlier for a holiday at home and the British High Commissioner had done likewise on 10 October. When I had drawn the British diplomat's attention to my apprehensions about growing differences between Nawaz and Musharraf, he had rather superciliously replied that he was sure that nothing momentous would happen when the American and British Heads of Mission were away from Islamabad!

12 October was the Spanish National day and I was preparing to leave for the national day reception at the Spanish Embassy residence, when Pakistan television announced that General Musharraf had been removed from office and the ISI Chief, Lieutenant General Ziauddin, appointed as the new army chief. I informed Foreign Secretary Raghunath and added that I did not think that the matter had simply ended with the announcement. Apart from anything else, Ziauddin was a Kashmiri officer from the Corps of Engineers and just did not enjoy the respect of persons like General Aziz Khan. Just as I was returning home to change for the reception, I saw khaki-clad soldiers of the Pakistan army in full battlegear climbing over the walls of the Pakistan Television Station from where the announcement of Musharraf's removal had come. I rushed back and informed Raghunath that the military was in the process of staging a coup to oust Nawaz. He asked me to check what had happened to Nawaz. I had already sent the Military Adviser, Brigadier Rakesh Das, and the Air Attaché, Group Captain Jaiswal, to check and let me know what was happening at Nawaz Sharif's residence and at the Presidential Palace. Other officers had been sent to different parts of Islamabad and Rawalpindi and told to get back within an hour. Barely an hour

later, I informed Brajesh Misra and Raghunath that the army had arrested Nawaz at his residence and surrounded the Presidential Palace. I added that it was only a question of time before the entire country was taken over by the army. This is precisely what happened, although there was some drama staged in Karachi before the Corps Commander, Lieutenant General Muzaffar Usmani, arrived at the airport and asserted his authority. A couple of days later, I asked General Mirza Aslam Beg how long it had taken him to stage such a coup by soldiers of the 111 Brigade, when Prime Minister Mohammed Khan Junejo was similarly dealt with in 1987. He told me that it had taken him some hours to get the soldiers ready to act after President Zia had given him the orders. The fact that the 111 Brigade had moved to act within minutes of the announcement ousting Musharraf from office clearly showed that meticulous advance preparation had been made for the take-over prior to Musharraf's departure for Colombo.

New Delhi was seriously concerned by the Musharraf takeover. And true to form, Musharraf did not bother to send any signals to reassure India that he had put his Kargil-type of adventurism behind him. His repeated rubbishing of the Lahore Declaration and endorsing of jihad in Kashmir only strengthened the view in Delhi that he was an incorrigible warmonger. The appointment of Abdul Sattar as Foreign Minister reinforced these misgivings. Sattar, who had been Pakistan's High Commissioner in Delhi and also served as Foreign Secretary, was a known hard-liner, who regarded the Simla Agreement as an unequal treaty imposed on a defeated nation. He was a member of the Tehriq-e-Insaf party in Pakistan. Even though this Party was ostensibly led by cricketer Imran Khan, its real moving force was known to be the hard-line Islamist, former ISI Chief, General Hamid Gul. Given New Delhi's decision to refuse to accord Musharraf any legitimacy, I had little chance to interact with the military hierarchy, though I kept in touch with Sattar and the new Foreign Secretary Inam ul Haq, who unlike his predecessor Shamshad Ahmad, was a sophisticated and savvy diplomat with a wry sense of humour. I also knew Musharraf's Information Adviser Javed Jabbar, Commerce Minister Razzaq Dawood and Agriculture Minister Shafkat Shah personally and there were occasions when meetings with these functionaries did give one an insight into what the regime was thinking. But New Delhi saw to it that the international pressure on Musharraf as a military dictator continued by forging a widespread consensus to exclude Pakistan from the Council of the Commonwealth.

worsening relations

It was in this situation that Indian Airlines Flight IC 814 was hijacked on 24 December 1999 when on a scheduled flight from Kathmandu to Delhi. I had handled two hijackings in 1984 when posted in Karachi and was pretty well aware of the Pakistani modus operandi in dealing with hijackings of Indian civil airlines aircraft. (It was during one of the hijackings in 1984 that was terminated in Dubai that the ISI actually provided a pistol to the hijackers at Lahore airport.) I informed Delhi that I expected that the flight would inevitably be taken to Lahore and got in touch with the Pakistan Foreign Office. When our authorities failed to terminate the hijacking at Amritsar the aircraft flew into Lahore. I asked the Pakistan Foreign Office to help me to get to Lahore, with Jaswant Singh reinforcing this request by speaking to Sattar. However, I made it clear to Jaswant Singh that I expected that the flight would be taken to Dubai, as the Pakistanis would refuse to let the aircraft stay in Lahore. Not surprisingly, this is precisely what happened. But not before the charade of endeavouring to take me to Lahore was enacted. It was over three hours after my initial request was made that the redoubtable Tariq Altaf landed up at the Rawalpindi air base to accompany me on a flight in a MI 17 Russian-built helicopter to Lahore. The engines of the helicopter had barely started when the pilot informed me that IC 814 had taken off from Lahore and asked if I still wanted to proceed to Lahore. Responding in disgust, I said: 'Obviously, no.' We soon learnt that true to form, the aircraft was headed for Dubai, where it landed a few hours later, after the Dubai authorities initially refused permission for landing. Sadly, over the years, our leaders, unlike Indira Gandhi, had lost personal contact with the leaders of Dubai and other Arab Gulf states. Unlike in 1984, when Dubai's ruler Sheikh Mohammed had personally intervened and ensured that the hijacking was terminated and the hijackers handed over to us, the authorities in Dubai behaved in a correct manner in dealing with the hijacking of IC 814, but not with the understanding they had shown in 1984. We have all too often neglected the need to maintain high-level personal contacts with the rulers of the Arab Gulf States, who are otherwise quite friendly to us.

In the early hours of the next morning, the number two man in the Taliban Embassy in Islamabad rang up our Political Counselor Ruchi Ghanshyam and informed her that he had received intimation that IC 814 was headed for Kandahar and asked what action the Taliban authorities should take. He was advised that the Taliban should allow the aircraft to land, and we would then decide how best to terminate the hijacking. It was interesting that the Taliban knew about the ultimate destination of IC 814 before we did. Once IC 814 landed in Kandahar, it became obvious that the Taliban authorities were not going to be merely disinterested intermediaries. It was their effort throughout the hijacking to appear to be keen on ending the hijacking, while actually endorsing what the hijackers demanded. The Taliban ambassador initially indicated to me that they were keen that the negotiations with the hijackers should be expeditiously concluded. They would otherwise allow the aircraft to be flown away from Kandahar. He urged that a team of officials should fly to Kandahar from Delhi to negotiate the release of the passengers and aircraft. I told him flatly that there was no question of anyone coming from Delhi till we were informed about the identity of the hijackers. After a series of exchanges on the subject and on my refusing to yield to the Taliban embassy's suggestion for an early arrival of a team of Indian negotiators in Kandahar, the Taliban Embassy informed us that the leader of the hijackers had come out of the aircraft. The Taliban representative told me that the hijacker had indicated that he was Ibrahim, the brother of a leader of the Harkat-ul-Mujahideen, its ideologue, Maulana Masood Azhar, who was then under arrest in India. The hijackers were all Pakistani nationals. I must mention that I was disappointed by the fact that even as I was talking to Taliban officials, I found that officials in Delhi were also trying to talk to them directly. I felt that not only was this counterproductive but that it also undermined my credibility with Taliban interlocutors.

In the meantime, a well-known Pakistani journalist in Peshawar, who was known to have close ties with the Taliban and direct access to Mullah Omar and the Taliban leadership, contacted me. We thus had two tracks of contacts with the Taliban—the first with the Taliban Embassy and the second through the journalist in Peshawar who conveyed messages to us directly from Mullah Omar's headquarters in Kandahar. Throughout the hijacking, it was evident that given the close ties between the Harkat-ul-Mujahideen on the one hand and the ISI and the Taliban on the other, the negotiations were going to be tough. This indeed turned out to be the case. While the Taliban kept insisting that our team should arrive without further delay, I insisted that the Taliban should first give us a firm assurance that should the hijackers harm any of the passengers, they would storm the aircraft. In the meantime, hysterical relatives of some of the passengers ran amuck in Delhi, weeping and screaming publicly and demanding that the Government should be prepared to meet the demands of the hijackers to get their relatives released. Indian and international television networks were carrying all this worldwide. The Taliban kept constantly telling me that the passengers of the aircraft were recalling how we had freed Kashmiri terrorists in 1990 to secure the release of Rubaiyya Sayeed, the kidnapped daughter of the then Union Home Minister, Mufti Mohammed Sayeed. The Taliban asserted that the passengers were saying that the only reason the Indian Government was not agreeing to the demands of the hijackers that included the release of arrested terrorists and millions of dollars as ransom in cash, was that there was no relative of any influential Minister or VIP in the aircraft.

Throughout my negotiations with the Taliban, I made it clear that there was no way that we would agree to release jailed terrorists to secure the release of the aircraft and passengers. I categorically told them that we had learnt from the mistakes made during the Rubaiyya Sayeed episode and would not yield to demands of terrorists. I kept reminding them of their assurance that they would storm the aircraft if even one passenger were harmed. When the threat was held out that the Taliban would allow the aircraft to leave Afghanistan, I told them that they knew better than anyone else that the hijackers had nowhere to go. Pakistan would be too embarrassed to let the aircraft land on any of its airfields. And India had excellent relations with both the Iranians and the Arabs. But I could sense that New Delhi was getting increasingly impatient and wanted the hijacking to end before the advent of the twenty-first century. Some of our private television channels were covering the entire episode in a manner that can only be described as irresponsible.

The Taliban and their Pakistani mentors evidently concluded, and rightly so, that it was only a question of time before New Delhi would yield to the demands of the hijackers. On 28 December, I was told that I would have no further role in negotiations with the Taliban. A team of middle-level officials without a clearly defined command structure or mandate was haphazardly and hastily put together and was sent to Kandahar where our Commercial Counselor, A.R. Ghanshyam (whose wife Ruchi was the Political Counselor in the High Commission), had already arrived. Ghanshyam later told me how the Taliban's actions in Kandahar were guided and controlled by Urdu-speaking Pakistanis. He also recounted how one of the hijackers was brought to the aircraft in the car used by Foreign Minister Mukil Ahmed Mutawakil in order to identify and unload the baggage that had been checked in by the hijackers. Mercifully, I ensured that every conversation that my colleagues and I had with people in Delhi and with others involved in the hijacking episode including Taliban representatives was meticulously recorded and ultimately sent to the CBI even before criminal investigations into the hijacking commenced.

The final act in the Kandahar hijack drama was enacted on 31 December 1999, the last day of the twentieth century. Three hard-core terrorists, Mushtaq Zargar, who was regarded as a psychopath involved in brutal terrorist killings in the Kashmir valley, Maulana Masood Azhar, an ideologue committed to the destruction of the Indian Union, and Syed Omar Sheikh, detained for kidnapping American tourists near Delhi, were released to meet the demands of the hijackers. Mushtaq Zargar today fans militancy and terrorist violence from across the Line of Control in Jammu and Kashmir. Maulana Masood Azhar heads a terrorist outfit, the Jaish-e-Mohammad, that staged the terrorist attack on the Indian Parliament on 13 December 2001. Syed Omar Sheikh awaits the execution of the death penalty awarded to him for his involvement in the brutal murder of American journalist Daniel Pearl. What was even worse was that these terrorists were taken to Kandahar in an aircraft carrying External Affairs Minister, Jaswant Singh.

According to those who travelled on the aircraft in which Jaswant Singh travelled to Kandahar along with the three released terrorists, Maulana Masood Azhar spent his time on the flight to Kandahar hurling abuses at Jaswant Singh and India. No incident has symbolized the surrender and the abdication of authority of the Indian State since the release of terrorists during the Rubaiyya Sayeed kidnapping more than the manner in which we bowed to terrorist demands during the Kandahar hijacking. Even Ministers in the Government in Delhi were shocked at Jaswant Singh travelling on the same aircraft to Kandahar as a group of hard-core terrorists. When a senior Cabinet Minister in Delhi asked me whether I felt that it was necessary for the External Affairs Minister to have travelled with terrorists to Kandahar, I responded by saying that it would be inappropriate for a High Commissioner to comment on an action of his Foreign Minister. In Pakistan, this action was seen as a confirmation of the belief of the military/intelligence establishment that India is a soft state.

I was told by an Israeli friend that the main reason for our abject surrender at Kandahar was information we had received that the hijackers were prepared to blow up the aircraft and kill the passengers if we failed to accede to their demands. I have, however, no reason to believe that the already internationally discredited Taliban would have allowed this to happen. I also do not understand why we never made public the Taliban assurance conveyed to me that they would storm the aircraft if the passengers were harmed. This would certainly have reassured the relatives of the passengers and also compelled the Taliban to keep a check on what the hijackers did.

My tenure as High Commissioner in Islamabad did help my wife and I to renew old friendships in Karachi and strike new ones in Lahore and Peshawar. But the entire atmosphere was tense and even people from well-known and highly respected families were apprehensive about meeting us. There were at least three instances when we were invited to dinner by very well known business people in Karachi, only to learn later that our hosts had been intimidated and harassed by the ISI. Some of the most influential business families in Lahore were similarly treated for merely being hospitable and friendly to us. Much as we would have liked to renew many of our old acquaintances we refrained from doing so out of the apprehension that even Pakistanis whom we had known well earlier, and who were well respected in society, would be harassed for being friendly to us. The days when we could spend long musical evenings together with friends in Karachi had become a rarity. But the journalists in Karachi remained a gutsy crowd and, unlike in Islamabad and Lahore, the ISI did not appear to have infiltrated the newspaper establishments in Karachi. It was not difficult to locate ISI operatives working as journalists in Islamabad and Lahore. One could sense their presence by the obvious distaste that their colleagues, who were genuine journalists, had for them.

Despite these complications, it was a pleasure to associate with and get to know people of great integrity and courage like Asma Jehangir, I.A. Rehman, Faqir Aijazuddin and Brigadier Rao Abid in Lahore and many people in Peshawar who entertained warm feelings for India. Families like those of Syed Babar Ali or former Commerce Minister Razak Dawood do recognize the importance of ending confrontation with India. But they have to be careful in differing too much from the conventional wisdom of the military elite in Punjab. The Wali Khan family still played an important role on the political scene in the North West Frontier Province and was very highly regarded. The media in Peshawar were also lively and independent. They were naturally more interested in developments in Afghanistan than they were about events in Kashmir. But in the North West Frontier Province also, one could sense a growing spread of Islamization in day-to-day life. Shanti and I were also delighted to renew friendships with many of those whom we had known so well in better times in Karachi.

The political scene in Pakistan after the Musharraf coup was no different from what it was when General Zia ruled the country in the 1980s. Within a few weeks of the coup of 12 October, a number of Muslim League leaders started telling me how Nawaz Sharif had proved a disaster for the country and that General Musharraf would soon bring back democracy. Families of the feudal elite have invariably behaved like this whenever there is a military takeover. There were many politicians who, while claiming to be Sindhi or Baluchi nationalists, were always amongst the first to cosy up to any new military ruler. The electorate, more often than not, punishes turncoats in India. Sadly this does not happen often enough in Pakistan. It was precisely such manoeuvrings that led to honest and decent political leaders like Sherbaz Khan Mazari quitting politics in disgust. But the one experience that will always remain in my mind is the fear and uncertainty that gripped the minds of ordinary Pakistanis when the army seized power on 12 October 1999.

Just before I took over in Islamabad I made it clear to everyone in Delhi whom I met that there had been far too many instances of our officers and staff in Islamabad getting beaten up. I recalled that this used to happen in the early 1980s till we made it clear that there would be swift retaliation in Delhi. Throughout the 1990s, members of the staff of our High Commission were beaten up almost routinely and we failed to take any action, apart from registering a diplomatic protest. There is a fairly routine manner in which this happens. On some occasions, the ISI incites Sikh separatists from UK, USA and elsewhere to create circumstances in which violence is unleashed against liaison officers from the High Commission accompanying Sikh pilgrims. Ravindranthan, an attaché in our High Commission, was beaten up and hospitalized just after the Lahore Summit. I knew Nawaz Sharif disapproved of such actions. We came to the conclusion that General Javed Nasir had engineered the incident, as the former ISI Chief was then masterminding efforts to subvert and incite Sikh pilgrims. But the second incident I faced was like others that had regularly taken place in the recent past.

Around 75 per cent of the staff of the Pakistan High Commission in Delhi has ISI links and actively participates in espionage, involving the subversion of Indian citizens, to obtain classified information. Pakistan High Commission staff members are not infrequently caught red-handed along with their Indian contacts. Unlike the Indian Military Attaché in Islamabad who spends all his time in assessments and open contacts, the Pakistan Military Attaché in the High Commission in Delhi is also the boss of the ISI set up in the Mission. Those who have been caught red-handed in acts of espionage in India include such notables as the former Military Attaché, Brigadier Abbassi. (Brigadier Abbassi was later, as a commander in Siachen, to mount suicidal attacks on our troops—attacks which were beaten back with heavy Pakistani casualties. He finally ended up under arrest for attempting to stage an Islamist coup against the Benazir Bhutto Government, only to be pardoned by an obliging General Musharraf.) In most cases, the state police arrests those involved in espionage. They are then handed over to the Union Government security agencies before the External Affairs Ministry and the Pakistan High Commission are informed. The Pakistan diplomat concerned is released as soon as the Pakistan High Commission is informed. News of such arrests often reaches the Indian media. The Pakistan Deputy High Commissioner is then summoned to the Foreign Office and asked to withdraw the official concerned within seven days.

Soon after the return of the expelled Pakistani official to Islamabad, reports start appearing authored by the so-called 'Special Reporting Cell' in the Urdu newspaper, *Jang* (which often bases its stories on ISI briefings) suggesting that Indian High Commission officials are involved in subversion. This is generally followed by the kidnapping and severe beating up of an Indian High Commission official, who is then asked to leave the country. This is precisely what happened when a Pakistani official was caught in the first week of June 1999 receiving classified information from an Indian contact who had worked for a paramilitary force. Anticipating retaliation, I had instructed all my staff members not to walk or travel alone, but in groups. Despite this, ISI agents forcibly abducted one of our officials in the presence of his screaming wife and his protesting Pakistani neighbours. The ISI goons also beat up the Indian security guard accompanying him. The official's wife was naturally hysterical as her husband suffered from a heart ailment. It was after repeated personal protests pointing out the medical condition of the official that he was released. But only after he was severely beaten and bruised.

I had expected an incident like this to take place and had repeatedly and strongly told Delhi that it would be impossible for me to retain the trust, confidence and respect of my staff unless there was retaliation that was swift and more than proportionate. Barely half an hour after the abduction in Islamabad, two Pakistan High Commission staffers were picked up by unknown persons in South Delhi and given a sound thrashing, that led to their being admitted to hospital. The Pakistan High Commissioner in Delhi, Ashraf Qazi, tried his best to get the Indian media to meet his staff members and give coverage to the incident. I was relieved that New Delhi had anticipated this and suitably explained the background to our media. Ashraf Qazi could not get any sympathy from even the normally obliging sections of our media. Similarly, when we complained to the Foreign Office in Islamabad that ISI agents following Political Counselor Ruchi Ghanshyam, a gutsy and competent Bhopal University Graduate, were passing lewd comments about her no action was taken. A few days later, the First Secretary in the Pakistan High Commission, a lady diplomat who was a very friendly person, genuinely interested in Indian art and culture, found the windscreen of her car smashed to bits, when the car was parked at a new Delhi hotel. The message got home. The ISI agents trailing Ruchi were quietly changed and at least while I was High Commissioner in Islamabad, my staff breathed freely, confident that the ISI would think twice before manhandling them.

prospects

My last few months in Islamabad were spent in seeing if anything could be done to bring the relationship back on track. A large number of politicians and others close to Musharraf were sounded out to ascertain whether the General, who had assumed the odd designation of Chief Executive of Pakistan, was willing to honour past Pakistani commitments made by democratically elected Governments in Simla and Lahore. The message I got was that General Musharraf and his Foreign Minister, Abdul Sattar, not only remained adamant in not ending support for their jihad in Kashmir, but they also had no inclination to honour past agreements. When I tried to raise the issue of trade and economic ties and the need for moving ahead on economic cooperation and integration bilaterally and regionally with Sattar, his response was caustic, suggesting that he did not see any potential for such cooperation. My farewell call on General Musharraf was similarly disappointing. When I mentioned to him that we had been encouraged by his references to de-weaponization of Pakistani society and that we hoped that in keeping with his stated policies, groups like the Lashkar-e-Taiba and the Harkat-ul-Mujahideen would be disarmed, he beat a hasty retreat from what he had stated earlier and claimed that his aim was to end sectarian violence within Pakistan.

Life in Pakistan had changed immensely in the period between my first and second tenures there. There was a sense of cynicism that permeated vast sections of society about anything that any ruler or the Government said. Economic conditions had changed drastically. In the 1980s, Pakistan had a growing economy. The influx of the gun culture and the extensive weaponization of Pakistani society had made cities like Karachi increasingly unsafe. Foreign investment had dried up and the stock market remained in the doldrums. Rich Pakistanis were spiriting their money away abroad. More importantly, many of our friends who in the 1980s were educating their children abroad in the clear expectation that they would return home to new job opportunities, were now only talking about how to send their children to settle down in foreign lands. Amidst all this, there was a military establishment that had grandiose ideas about how it could destabilize and dismember India. It was an unreal world in Islamabad talking to former Generals who somehow believed that Pakistan had an indispensable role to play in the advancement of the Islamic Ummah. The word 'introspection' seemed to be absent from the lexicon of the military establishment. I had always feared that it was India that would find it very difficult to adjust to the realities of the post-Cold War, economically globalized world order. While we adjusted soon to the new situation, Pakistan sadly lacked the leadership or people with vision to recognize that the days of its presumed indispensability to the western world were over. The leadership in Pakistan just ignored that it was for them to create an environment that would attract foreign investment and promote human development. Instead of prioritizing these tasks, all the country's woes were attributed either to a malevolent India or an ungrateful United States.

Pakistan is today at the crossroads of its history. It can either choose the path of giving primary importance to issues of economic and human development or continue with its present policies of confrontation with India, advocacy of jihad and worldwide Islamic causes. If it chooses the former path, then India should be prepared to reciprocate. Pakistan does after all have an immense wealth of talented and resourceful people. It is located on river basins that have historically made it the richest part of the sub-continent agriculturally. It can serve as a point of transit for the vast resources of gas that India will need in the coming years from the Persian Gulf and Central Asia. With imaginative diplomacy, based on the belief that economic integration unites peoples and countries in common endeavours, solutions can be found to issues like Jammu and Kashmir.

India in turn will have to shed its overly protectionist policies and be more generous than it has hitherto been in granting market access to its smaller neighbours. We also need to be far less paranoid about Pakistanis visiting India, either as tourists, or to meet their friends and relatives. As a mature and self-confident democracy, we have to recognize that nothing is going to change mindsets in Pakistan about us more than visits by Pakistanis to our country. Pakistan will have to be persuaded by firm action on our part that it can either chose the path of prosperity through increasing regional economic integration in South Asia or face economic stagnation and international suspicion by continuing on its present path of encouraging the promotion of jihad in its neighbourhood and seeking to destabilize India. There is mercifully now some recognition in Pakistan that while the United States will continue to humour it and shower it with economic assistance in the aftermath of the events of 9/11, this free lunch will end, sooner rather than later, as it has in the past. I sincerely hope that we can see Pakistan moving in the direction of moderation and economic development in the not-too-distant future. But over two decades of dealing with Pakistan, and especially its military establishment, has persuaded me that the path ahead is going to be neither easy nor simple.

There is now growing recognition in Pakistan of the strength and resilience of Indian democracy. But we will have to constantly remember that while many of the problems we now face in Jammu and Kashmir and elsewhere may be accentuated by Pakistani malevolence, we cannot ignore the fact that we have ourselves allowed narrow political considerations and poor governance to create situations that Pakistan has naturally exploited. The problems in Punjab could well be attributed to the communalization of politics there. And we would have to recognize that many of those who took to arms in Jammu and Kashmir in the 1980s and thereafter did so after they got the feeling that the democratic processes in the State were flawed and elections rigged. More recently, the carnage that followed the Godhra massacre in Gujarat was politically encouraged and supported. When will we learn that polarizing people on communal lines or undermining democratic institutions, especially in border states, is a recipe for disaster? With the increasing communalization and criminalization of politics in India, our media and civil society institutions have a crucial role to play in ensuring that we do not repeat the mistakes of the past and that the high ideals of pluralism and secularism enshrined in our Constitution are not eroded.

The communal violence in Gujarat has enabled the Pakistan army to tell its people that minorities and, especially Muslims, cannot live in safety and security in India. India will prevail in its ideological battle over Pakistan only when the values of democracy, pluralism and secularism enshrined in its Constitution are seen to be more enduring than Mohammad Ali Jinnah's advocacy of Muslim separatism. At the same time, there is no scope for complacency, sentimentalism, or undue optimism in dealing with the military establishment in Pakistan. General Musharraf and his associates, like General Aziz Khan, have made it clear that relations with India will continue to be tense and marked by 'low intensity conflict' even if the Kashmir issue is resolved. Kashmir is thus merely a symptom and not the root cause of the problems we face in dealing with a military establishment in Pakistan whose very existence, powers, perks and privileges require it to adopt a policy of compulsive and continuing hostility towards India.